the sec

the second half

HUNTER DAVIES

POMONA

A POMONA BOOK P-013
Mad in England!

Published by Pomona 2006

1 3 5 7 9 8 6 4 2

Pomona Books
PO Box 50, Hebden Bridge, West Yorkshire HX7 8WA, England, UK
Telephone 01422 846900 · e-mail ursula@pomonauk.co.uk
www.pomonauk.co.uk

Distribution: Central Books Ltd., 99 Wallis Road, London E9 5LN
Telephone 0845 458 9911 · Fax 0845 458 9912
e-mail orders@centralbooks.com · www.centralbooks.com

Reps: Troika, United House, North Road, London N7 9DP
Telephone 020 7619 0800

A CIP catalogue record for this book
is available from the British Library

ISBN 1-904590-14-4

Typeset in Granjon
by Christian Brett

Printed and bound in England by Cox & Wyman

the second half

Introduction

A SEASON IS A LONG TIME IN FOOTBALL. LET'S SAY you went off to Mars for nine months, or set off to catch the Carlisle train from Euston, or became a member of the House of Lords, anything really that is liable to cut you off from modern civilisation for a considerable period, then when you came back, you'd be very confused by what has happened in your absence, footer wise.

Players who were household names in your house will have disappeared—and now be wearing the shirt of a hated rival. Boy managers you've never heard of will be on the touch-line, as if they belonged there, screaming abuse through their dummies, at the dummies. Foreign players, previously unknown and with unpronounceable names, will have become fans' pets, given affectionate nicknames, become one of us, or not, as the case is more likely to be.

A new owner, fresh out of Siberia or Dartmoor, has taken over, introduced dancing girls when the team comes out and cheap Bulgarians, passing through, on the way back to Bulgaria, or the Conference. A hitherto useless, joke team is in your division, and wasn't there last season. How did they make it? And doing rather well, while that long established, solid looking club, pillar of the Top Leagues since 1888, winner of bla bla, is now playing in the, well, somewhere, Gawd, what do they call that league now? Nottingham Forest, yeh, what happened to them? Don't say they're now called Milton Keynes Robin Hood Dons.

Shirt sponsors, their names are likely to change between games, sometimes even at half-time. Stadiums get re-christened while you're not watching and it's hopeless trying to keep up with the, er, Carling Cup, no hold on, Worthington Cup. It's not still the Milk Cup is it? Help.

So it has been rather weird sitting down quietly and looking over these pieces I have been trotting out for the *New Statesman* over these last three years, another collection which Pomona Books has decided to publish. The first one did so incredibly well that they think they can pull off the same trick.

When they suggested it, I said "not now Bernard." (The Pomona boss is, in fact, called Mark, but in our house we always say Not Now Bernard, a reference to a book all our children loved).

Three years since the last collection seemed a bit quick, not much will have happened, but when I started re-reading, it has, to my surprise.

Abramovich, no sign of him three years ago. Chelsea looked doomed never to do anything much, for ever. Arsenal still had several English players playing for them, hard to believe now. Hoddle was managing Spurs, or have I made that up? Seems centuries ago. Roy Keane was still in his pomp for Man Utd. Paul Scholes was being excellent for England. Beckham was going to, well, where was he going to? we all wondered, sensing that Fergie had had enough of him. Sven, surely he would get the push as he clearly had no idea what he was doing and only appeared to summon up any full blooded energy and enthusiasm when it came to extra-curricular activities.

These three years have also included two major tournaments—the Euro Nations in Portugal in 2004 and the World Cup in Germany in 2006. In writing about these, and other topics, week by week, reacting like any other fan on the terraces or in front of the telly, I naturally got a lot of things wrong, made some really stupid comments, offered wild predictions, expressed extreme hatred. Like most fans, really. I haven't changed them, or doctored them. That was how we felt, or I felt, that week, at that moment in time.

During these three years, my own life has gone on much the same—following both Spurs and Arsenal in London and while in Lakeland, where we spend the summer half of the year, supporting Carlisle United. And what a remarkable three years CUFC have had. Down, up, up. Amazing. I certainly didn't predict that.

From a work point of view, among many exciting new books, I also wrote Gazza's autobiography, which sold shitloads and won a big prize. And then in my *NS* column, having mocked the very idea of Wayne Rooney, aged 20, being signed up for five volumes of autobiography, I found myself being asked to do it. Yes, football, funny old game. You have to laugh. Which I hope you will...

Hunter Davies,
Loweswater, August 2006

2003–04
SEASON

Becks gets Real,
Me and Gazza,
who do you fancy—
Fergie or Wenger?

Imagine Branson giving his trillions to a Russian hot-air balloon team

8 September 2003

OH, IT'S SO GREAT TO BE BACK, LIFE RETURNING AS we know it, football life that is, what else is there. And it's so exciting this season, more news, more fun. More to look forward to than I can ever remember at this stage. Which isn't saying much. Once a season departs, it plops into a grey hole in my mind where all the seasons become one, everyone plays for the same team, with George Best on the wing, Jimmy Greaves goal-hanging, Big George Young being big at the back, Frank Swift guarding the net, Alf Common has just been transferred and Preston North End are invincible.

Flicking back through 115 years since 1888 and the beginning of the world's first footer season, which was when I started following, I can't think of two bigger pre-season shock-horror stories. Namely, Abramovich arriving and Beckham departing.

If I were a Russian footer fan, or a Russian taxpayer, or in the Russian government, I'd be well pissed off with him taking all his easy-gotten, jammy, dodgy billions overseas to play with, lavishing it on flashy, foreign tarts. It's our money, they must all be moaning, why can't they spend it on us?

Imagine Richard Branson going off with his trillions to settle in Russia and run his own hot-air balloon team, or the Duke of Westminster selling off all the English counties he inherited to invest in some naked Chinese female wrestlers. How would we feel? Since you mention it, quite pleased, actually.

Beckham — now that is an even more pleasing story, with legs, made for running. I never thought he'd leave. Then, after that first game against Real Mallorca, I thought that's it, he's blown it, taken off and humiliated, he won't even make it as a water carrier, a poseur in search of a role, a coat-hanger without a wardrobe, he'll end up as peripheral as he was last season at Man Utd, what a mistake, poor petal, cuddle him before he cries.

Then blow me, he scores in two minutes on his league debut against Real Betis and is instantly back as the fancy Dan, cock of the walk, we all know he can be. I predict that's how it will go on. Up and down, you owe me half a crown.

It's quite taken the edge off this season's other excitements such as the return of long hair. I really did think Hernan Crespo was a tart when I saw his Chelsea arrival photo. These foreign johnnies do love the long locks — eg, Amoruso, Tugay, Angel, Berger, Viana, Petit, Pires, Forlan. The reaction of our English chaps is to shave even closer to the bonce. I think little Micky Owen will eventually disappear if he has it done again.

Only Robbie Savage of our native Premiership beasts has long hair, but of course he's Welsh. Savage has also provided one of the season's best images so far, when he got elbowed in the face in the Birmingham-Newcastle game and went down as if dead. I was half dozing at the time, thinking, now, which side is playing in green, then I realised it was the referee wot had clobbered him. God, that was funny, at least to supporters of any team that Savage has ever played against.

I haven't got used to players playing for teams they don't belong to, such as Damien Duff turning out for Chelsea. So far, it hasn't changed him. He still has that stiff, stick-like walk, which he shares with Roy Keane. Are they by chance related? Or is it an Irish trait, an Irish gait?

They still haven't got the electronic board things sorted, with fourth officials continuing to be dazed and confused every time they try to hold one up. What have they been doing all summer? Couldn't they have had lessons?

A new arrival at Blackburn Rovers is a horde of hoardings for Air Mauritius which I'm sure were not there last season. What is the point? Must be that on leaving Ewood Park, after a pint and a pie, the lads now say, I know, let's get a flight to Mauritius.

But the best image of the season so far was in that Real Madrid-Real Betis game when a streaker came on. He stripped off naked, except for some Christmas-tree golden balls attached to his cock. It took me at least three minutes to get the significance. (A homage to Becks's Man Utd nickname, of course, which in Spain has become "Bolas de Oro".)

Go thump him, I said, let someone else do the sodding commentary

15 September 2003

FOOTBALL DOMINATES MY LIFE, THINGS REVOLVE around it. I organise it either to be given precedence or fit in, whether it's with my social life, working life, family stuff.

Oh no, we can't go for lunch on Sunday, ever again, yes I know they are our best friends, but don't you realise there's a live game at two and another at four. Not the next few Saturdays either, lunch or supper, 'cos I'm going in to Carlisle to watch CUFC and I need to set off early. Or Saturdays after that; I'll either be at Spurs or Arsenal. Nor any Monday, Tuesday, Wednesday or Friday. I haven't paid a fortune to Sky in order not to watch whatever there is to watch, whether Portuguese under-12s or Albanian over-60s. Thursday? Hmm, now then. Perhaps. Not saying which Thursday, don't get excited, or which year, but there could well be an empty Thursday, some time between now and, well, death. I don't fear death. I just look upon it as the end of the final football season.

Sometimes, though, when I'm not looking, failing to pay proper attention, life creeps up on the outside and overtakes football. Which was why last Saturday, at half-time in the

Macedonia-England game, I had to leave my seat in front of the telly, get in the car and drive all the way to Penrith.

By then, they were one down. I had the most awful headache and my throat was sore with shouting at our crap players. Becks you're a fairy, Rooney get back in your nappy, Lampard, our tortoise is faster, Campbell, what are you doing you big lump. Not the best state in which to give a talk to 220 people.

Six months ago, I agreed to give the inaugural lecture at the Wainwright Society, a new organisation devoted to the works of the Blessed Wainwright, something I had long wanted to happen. Without realising what else would be on 6 September.

I caught most of the second half in the car, as I tore along the A66 to Rheged, where the lecture was to be given. All my youth, I listened to football on the radio, as there was no alternative, my little ears almost inside it. I always imagined I could see the movements, understand the sequence of events. I'm sure they painted much better word pictures in those days.

Today, it's mostly shouting, ending in the word "GOAL-LLLL!". Very often they miss the build-up, so busy giving us extraneous info. In that game, Alan Green kept on about some Macedonian yobbo he could see making racist chants whom he wanted to throttle. We, the listeners, couldn't see or even hear him, so I was shouting to Alan, go off and thump him, let someone else do the sodding commentary. But I picked up that England were almost as useless as in the first-half, just managing a jammy win.

Now it's happened again, twice in one week. I'm going

to be away for the England-Liechtenstein game which, as I write, is on Wednesday. I'll be in Newcastle, staying at the Malmaison, treating my dear wife to a cultural few days. I do spoil her. She's going to the Baltic and various other galleries. I'll be in Gateshead, best part, visiting Gazza's birthplace. I wonder if they've got a plaque up yet. I'm writing his autobiography, which was the real reason for this trip, though I'm pretending otherwise.

Somehow, I agreed to the date without checking the England diary. What am I doing? It must have been this long hot summer in Lakeland, best for years, all that swimming, softening my bonce. I'm hoping there will be a TV in our bedroom, but when I mentioned this, idly, in passing, she said if so, that was it, she wouldn't be going anywhere, ever again.

It will, in a way, be quite a cultural trip for me, too, as I have a very knowledgeable guide. I have his name in front of me, from a cutting in *Corriere dello Sport* dated 17 Maggio 1995.

In writing about Gascoigne, then playing for Lazio, they refer to "il suo amico Jimmy Cinquepance". I don't know whether they have satirically translated his nickname, or perhaps think it was his real one, but I'm sure you know who he is. Otherwise you haven't been alive these past ten years and putting footer first in your life...

Whole channels are devoted to football, but books get just two radio progs

22 September 2003

THIS IS APPALLING, SAID MY WIFE, SOUNDING LIKE Prince Charles. Why oh why, she continued, sounding like the *Daily Mail*, do we have to have all these acres devoted to football? The literary pages have practically disappeared. Even *The Sunday Times* doesn't have a separate book section any more.

I've changed our Monday newspaper from the Indy to *The Times*, purely because of their footer section, The Game, which really is fab, so much for healthy boys and girls to enjoy. In the past ten years, there has been an explosion in football coverage, especially in the broadsheets. Every day, they devote more actual words, as opposed to pics and headlines, to football than the tabloids.

Poor old lit eds. She, for it is usually a she, has to survive on an ever-shrinking space, on her own in a cubby-hole, whereas every sports editor has an army at his command, big budgets, dozens of pages. On radio and TV, it's even more pronounced. I can think of only two radio progs, and not one on TV, solely devoted to books—*A Good Read* and *Open Book* on Radio 4. With football, there are whole channels, whole stations.

Football has now muscled in on the books pages, such as they are. There's an esoteric Italian novel by Luther Blissett, remember him? Well, it's not him. They've just used his name, but it shows the influence of football.

In the current bestseller lists, hardback and paperback, there are six football books, something I can't remember happening before. The Becks book we can understand, but look at Nobby Stiles, not kicked a ball in decades, never exactly a pin-up, yet his book is up there with Martin Amis. (Last week's *Sunday Times* reported 1,190 in the week for Nobby, 1,835 for Mart.)

Writing about football is as old as football. Even before there was a Football League, there were books and annuals written by gentlemen for other gentlemen, often beautifully produced, fit to grace any country-house library. Once the League began, in 1888, a new activity and breed of human appeared—football reporters. Newspapers, which had devoted their sports pages solely to racing, increased their sales fourfold by reporting football. The first known press box was created in 1894 by Celtic. Until then, hacks didn't get much help. HAH Caton, one of the earliest football writers, who wrote under the name of Tityrus, betraying his classical background, remembered a game in Nottingham in 1883 where he had to stand behind the goals, but he was able to interview the goalie—during the match, while the game was going on.

Once it became a mass game, played by professionals, the working classes took over and the gents retired. Purple prose was saved for cricket while football writing got poorer, the books more cheaply produced. But fascinating none the less. From the 1920s onwards, in the popular football prints, you can read behind-the-scenes stuff about our heroes, their domestic life, their clothes, their likes and dislikes, just the sort of stuff Becks is dishing up today.

Football books did not sell well—just newsprint, the pink 'uns and green 'uns—but they did exist. Stars produced ghosted autobiographies, like David Jack in the 1930s and Len Shackleton in the 1950s. Mostly they were pretty anodyne, though Shack had a good dig at directors. His chapter about what directors know about football was blank.

What has changed today? Why do footer books sell so well? Football is at its most popular for 20 years, judging by attendances. But you now have to be well off, to have a season ticket or subscribe to Sky, so modern fans can well afford to buy proper books. They are also, in theory, more middle class, the sort who always had books in the house, and who have more of an interest in football history.

Well, that's what I like to think.

Carlisle win a point, and the sheep celebrate all over Cumbria

29 September 2003

I WENT TO CARLISLE UNITED'S FIRST GAME OF THE season, which was at home against York City. Our lads were two down in ten minutes and the York supporters, who must have numbered at least two carloads, started shouting: "Going down, going down." Cheeky beggars. But then that's how it's been for the past five seasons, with CUFC only ever escaping the ultimate drop at the last moment. After nine games, they're bottom again. I prefer to stand on my head to look at the table. It looks so much better.

Why do so many still turn up? Even stranger, why would anyone want to be a director? In the Premiership, the perks are obvious, pride enormous, civic and social influence tremendous. Down in the Third Division, it must be like doing third-world charity work.

As it happened, I sat with the directors for that York game, and had tea and buns at half-time in their lounge where, I could hardly believe it, there was air-conditioning. Well, it was 90 degrees that day. Which is now even harder to believe.

I was a guest of Lord Clark of Windermere, David Clark

as was, MP for South Shields for many years and a member of Blair's first cabinet as chancellor of the Duchy of Lancaster. He's an active life peer, chairman of the Forestry Commission, so why bother being a director of a potty little football club? He doesn't even live in Carlisle, but 40-odd miles away. Ah, but he's always supported them. His dad, who lived in Penrith, boasted that he was there for CUFC's first ever league game in 1928. (Against Accrington Stanley—Carlisle won 3–2; crowd: 6,714.) David, despite living in Windermere, has supported them for more than 40 years.

He was invited last year to join the new board, when the dreaded Michael Knighton eventually withdrew. He helped broker the new deal, though he has no money himself to put in. He reckoned he would be going to every home game anyway, and most of the northern ones, so it wouldn't take up too much more time, being a director. He likes travelling away in the team coach, getting to know the players. "That's when you discover their personalities. Some are so shy, others abrasive. They each need handling differently."

He didn't make it to Yeovil, now the longest journey in English football since Yeovil got promoted—but some directors did. The team took two days just to get there. So three days out of your life, just to watch Carlisle being stuffed again. I wouldn't do it if I was paid.

"We aren't, of course. None of the CUFC directors even charges expenses, though the team coach, of course, is free; and, if you stay with the team, so is the hotel." Such as it is. The club can afford only the cheapest Holiday Inn-type rooms, £40 max. He says the Third Division is full of equally dedicated directors, who spend a lot in time and money and take nothing.

In fact, he has put some money in. He sponsors the strip of striker Richie Foran, which cost him £400. "In return, Richie gave me one of his shirts, autographed. My daughter has it hanging on her wall in her home in Cockermouth." He also gets his name in the programme, plus two seats in the directors' box, with his own name on. So there are perks, even if it's not like being a Man Utd director.

"I want Carlisle to continue having a league team, now it's the last league club left in Cumbria. That's my main object. People do come from miles away, from all over the county, as far as Barrow. I think it matters to the community, for CUFC to survive.

"Being a director has turned out a bit like being an MP again, with my own constituency. For half an hour before every home match, I make a point of standing outside and talking to the fans, hearing their views and grievances, even if I can't tell them about everything going on." Such as happened a couple of weeks ago, when the board decided to sack the manager.

But last Saturday, CUFC did manage a point against Southend. Dancing round the old town hall. Sheep celebrating all over the county. Some time soon, this season, we might even manage a second win. Directors, like ordinary fans, live in hope.

Could Beckham be the first sentimental, soppy, touchy-feely manager?

6 October 2003

I'VE BEEN THINKING A LOT ABOUT HODDLE, ASKING many questions. As I'm sure he has. Could anyone have cared more about Spurs than I did, or worked harder? Which bastards knifed me in the back? Rebrov, I don't remember anyone called Rebrov? The very fact of asking himself such questions will show he is a long way from recovery. My question is about the nature of managership. Is the player father of the man?

I so admired Hoddle on the pitch, without knowing anything about his personality. On the field he appeared so confident, convinced of his skills, but he could also be lazy, uncommitted, fade away if he wasn't in the mood, or the occasion not worthy of him. He was such a natural, it had all come so easily, that I doubted if in real life he had much mental toughness or determination. I could not have been more wrong. Mental strength he clearly has, probably to excess. But his confidence on the field, which we consider essential and praiseworthy in a player, turned into cold arrogance as a manager, unable to allow other opinions.

In the 1980s, I could never have imagined him as a manager, so it has been astonishing that he has made a success of it. Managing three Premiership clubs, plus England, has to count as success. But has he been a great one? Most fans would say no.

He was unusual in being a star player who went on to do well in management. Looking at current Premiership managers—Fergie, Wenger, Houllier, Ranieri, David Moyes, Alan Curbishley, Dave Jones, Steve McClaren, Sam Allardyce, Micky Adams, Chris Coleman—none of those were household names as players. Well, not in my house. Steve Bruce was well known, at Man Utd, but not for England. Bobby Robson got 20 caps, but was never a star. Nor was Peter Reid, though he was well known. David O'Leary got lots of caps, but he was Irish. Graeme Souness and Gordon Strachan played for Scotland. The only ex-England star, on the Hoddle scale, now in Premiership management is Kevin Keegan. And his career has not exactly been brilliant.

Looking around the present Premiership stars, who will make it? You'd have to pick Roy Keane. He doesn't care about being popular, which is vital for every manager. Gary Neville appears solid and sensible. I can see Alan Shearer as a manager, and Teddy Sheringham, but will they want to slum it in the lower depths, or put up with the shit when it all goes wrong? With three or four million stashed away, they need never work again. That's another factor, which didn't figure in the past. Why be coach for Carlisle United when you can play golf all day.

The media also provide so much work, and lots of money, as Gary Lineker has discovered. And very much easier, with less chance of a heart attack. You needn't work at all, if you retire as an icon, and still earn money. George Best has made an excellent living for over 30 years, more than he did as a player, just by being George Best. Hard to imagine Beckham as a manager. He does so like to be liked, a terrible failing in that role. He also appears to lack any strong views, about football or anything else, judging by his latest autobiog. But you just can't tell. He could be our first soppy, sentimental, touchy-feely manager.

Almost all our Premiership managers in 20 years' time will be players we scarcely reckon or notice today. But a couple of present-day stars might come through, as Hoddle and Keegan did. My dear friend Gazza tells me he wants to be a manager, when he eventually retires. This is the player who sat at the back in England team meetings and burped, farted and made stupid noises while tactics were being explained. When players like Chris Waddle or John Barnes were discussing formations, Gazza would put his hands over his ears and shout: "Not listening, not listening."

I remember interviewing Terry Venables as a player and he mucked around, doing silly things with his eyebrows. Players do mature. Someone unexpected is bound to come through. They always do, in every field, from football to politics.

So, Gazza to get Hoddle's job at Spurs? That's pushing it. But one day, who knows.

You find girls' sizes, thongs in the club colours, knickers with cockerel patterns

13 October 2003

DID YOU READ THE NEW REPORT WHICH REVEALS that female fans now make up one-fifth of Premiership football crowds? No, I didn't either. All I read was a remark remarking on the report, third hand, possibly fifth hand, but that's not going to stop me commenting on it, with total confidence.

These surveys come out on the hour, often backed by commercial interests hoping for free publicity, knowing dozy or hard-up newspapers will pounce on them, highlighting one supposed fact out of context—and bingo, a whole page feature, based on, well, bugger all or something we all knew anyway.

On the subject of female fans, I happen to have done some in-depth research these past ten years. When standing in queues at Spurs, Arsenal or Carlisle, I automatically estimate the number of women. At Arsenal, you can very easily count in females wearing quite a bit of red who are, in fact, members of the Salvation Army, who gather at the West Stand with their collection boxes, probably been there since Queen Victoria.

When watching a boring match on telly, I concentrate on random crowd shots. I have trained my eyes to group people into batches of ten and instantly count the women. TV directors don't catch me. When it's truly boring, they focus in on pretty girls in the crowd, going back to them several times, depending how pretty and how revealing their clothes. I never count such shots. They are not, by definition, random.

And what is my conclusion, you ask, you cry, you demand? Well, the full report comes out soon, but here's the main finding—female fans make up only one-tenth of crowds. So sucks to that other dodgy, unscientific survey, overstating the situation.

But their main point is correct—the trend is for more and more female fans. Eventually, it could have a profound effect on the game. What you can't do, which many commentators did when pouncing on the other report, is suggest that it's all new.

I've spent a lot of time this past year on writing a history of football, which meant looking at loads of old photographs. Even in the earliest, from 1900, you can see female faces in the crowds. For big games, there were always women among the supporters who staggered or pranced around London wearing their team favours and silly hats. For the FA Cup Final of 1905, a group calling themselves the "Newcastle Ladies Final Outing Group" arranged their own trip to London, which rather surprised a writer for a local newspaper. "They had their own lady secretary, paid their own subscriptions and with the latter-day independence of their sex, came to London in their own saloon without the assistance or company of a single mere male."

I have a 1948 Manchester United brochure that pictures four very pretty Man U girl fans, with rosettes and scarves, who had made one of the biggest sacrifices any fan could make for their heroes. No, not that. They had pooled their sweetie rations to provide chewing gum for the lads.

Fifa predicts that by 2010, globally, there will be more women playing football than men. This is bound to increase the number of women going to games. Already, clubs have been forced to create more toilets for women. In the club shops, you find women's sizes in most items, thongs in club colours, knickers with cockerels on the front. (Not a schoolboy joke—it's the Spurs emblem.)

Football doesn't promote or advertise itself. It doesn't have to. Football is a vehicle for other products and services. As female fan numbers increase, a wider range of products will be attracted. I noticed last week a hoarding at Wolves for Wolverhampton Grammar School. Never seen an ad for a school at a game before. I suspect they had in mind family audiences.

Will women make crowds nicer? As, of course, women are nicer people. I haven't noticed less swearing or abuse, but my friend Sue, who lives two doors down from us and became a born-again Spurs fan five years ago, is always last back to the car. Almost every bloke has gone by the final whistle, some of them already home, still swearing, but she thinks it's discourteous not to wait and watch the players leave the pitch. Sweet.

Even in 1972, I knew of players passing a naked girl from room to room

20 October 2003

WHEN DID THINGS GO WRONG? WHY HAS FOOTBALL turned into a cesspit? Which is what the *Daily Mail* maintains. Have our footballers become morally depraved drunks, druggies and sexual beasts? Is football itself now totally corrupt? That has been the opinion of most people writing and talking about football these past few weeks. Why does Jonathan Pearce say "I seem to remember" while trotting out some idle, piddling fact, when you know he's got it written down in front of him?

That last question is a mystery, but all the others are easy to explain. Football has always been morally and financially corrupt. Right, I think that's cleared that up. Oh, when? I forgot to tell you when it all started.

About five past three o'clock on 8 September 1888. That's when the first professional season kicked off and the first shout of "My ball, ref" was heard from someone either lying, as he knew it was not his ball, or who had no idea whose ball it was but was trying to seek an advantage. From then on, the moral decline set in. Cheating, lying, injuring, diving, threatening, intimidating—all became a normal part of the game.

Traditionally, the English public school boys who gave us football played fair. Today, in a corner of every foreign field, or in the dressing room, you'll see a notice, in the local language, which includes the English words "fair play". From my knowledge of public school boys, they have always been as nasty, devious and cheating as anyone else, only smoother with it, but the myth lives on that football, as invented by English gentlemen, is meant to be played fairly.

The Corinthians, as amateurs, did try. When the opposition lost a man, for whatever reason, they would deliberately send off one of their own men, just to keep it fair and equal. Professionalism did away with all that nonsense.

It was around the same time, say 4.40pm on the first day of the first season, that the financial fiddles started. A proportion of the gate money would be kept back, undeclared, and used either to pay stars a bit extra, a few pound notes in their boots, or to persuade rival players to join them, with cash in their back pockets. Even when all the clubs agreed to abide by a maximum wage, or rigid transfer rules, they would still get round it. They didn't see it as morally wrong, or even corrupt. It was done for and justified by "the good of the club". Which is what they tell themselves today, when four or five million disappears during a big transfer deal, used to oil or pay off some dodgy agent or shadowy intermediary.

The sexual behaviour of players before the war was never made public, but we know there were always drunks and bad characters. Teams got invited on Saturdays after a game to the local music hall, plied with drink, paraded on stage, and if they had won, were cheered by all, including no doubt a few chorus girls.

Girls throwing themselves at footballers, such as George Best, appeared in the public prints from the 1960s. In 1972, I was aware of Spurs players passing a naked girl down a hotel corridor, from room to room. It didn't make the papers.

What's new today is the coverage. The tabloids, which in the past few weeks have been going tut tut, how disgusting, will pay up to £100,000 for a juicy kiss'n'tell, thereby encouraging dopey or cynical girls deliberately to target dopey or cynical footballers. The big wages in the Premiership are also new. Players *do* light joints with £50 notes, pour £300 bottles of champagne over each other's heads and see a £150,000 Ferrari as an impulse buy.

So is their moral behaviour getting worse? Not really. Do we care? Not a lot. Fans, like their managers, care most about what happens on the pitch, not off it. Playing shit, that's what really upsets us, not being a shit. The idea of them as role models is a laugh. That's not their job.

Will we now be put off watching football because we've been told, as if we didn't all know, that football is a cesspit? Leave it out.

Rugby, despite the hype, is less likely than ever to catch up with football

27 October 2003

THE ORGANISERS HAVE DONE A BRILLIANT JOB GETTING us all excited about the Rugby World Cup, masses of advertising, posters of hunks everywhere, endless interviews, slick TV previews. Bugger Beckham, Jonny Wilkinson is now the golden boy, master of the sporting universe, so look out soccer, you're shit and you know you are.

So naturally, I was full of anticipation as I settled down at lunchtime to watch England-South Africa, the first biggie, thinking if it's really good, I might not go to Arsenal. I did play rugby at school, and enjoyed it, and watch England and Scotland rugby internationals on the telly about five or six times per season. No one can say I'm prejudiced.

First surprise was Will Carling, sitting in the ITV studio, rugby's golden boy only yesterday. He's put on ten stone and 20 years since I last saw him. And there was Jim Rosenthal as well, wondered where he'd gone, an old folks' home, by the look of him. Don't people age when you're not watching them.

The England team still have huge necks, but are not as fat and beefy elsewhere as they used to be. Do they do neck exercises, or take neck steroids? Such a strange place to put on weight. Their new skin-tight shirts make them look less macho, more poofty, especially when they have to change their shirts and struggle like girls' blouses, literally, to get it over their fat necks.

I like the way rugby players get stuck in, thump each other, yet don't argue with the ref. Blood replacements are a good idea; so is being able to hear the ref. I enjoy the crowd singing "Sweet Chariot" and am amused by the nice public-school names such as Will Greenwood, Josh Lewsey, Dorian West. Not a Darren or a Wayne in sight. They are obviously fitter, quicker than they ever were and get all hyped up, desperately patriotic, singing their little hearts out during the National Anthem. Bless.

And yet, after 15 minutes, I was looking at my watch. I estimate that 40 per cent of the time in a rugby union game nothing is happening, at least nothing you can see happening, no sign of the ball, what with scrums and assorted mauling. So much is negative, like deliberately kicking the ball out.

Most of all, I hate penalties. I can't always understand why they are given, and the commentators don't help when they say it's a technical infringement. They are so often out of all proportion to the supposed crime, yet a side can win a game on penalties, like England, just by having a good kicker who doesn't miss. And they take so long, which at least means you can go to the lav, get a drink, wander round the garden, feed the wife, talk to the cat, and be back while the kicker is still placing the ball. Then he has to fix his hands, practise his mad stare.

In football, a penalty kicker is competing against another

human being. In rugby, it's against an inanimate object, a crossbar which can't move. What a nonsense. They might as well take the penalty kicks beforehand, on their own, before the game, in an empty stadium, and not bore us all.

We know there's a class difference, that in England rugby union is still played and followed by and large by the middle classes. That's partly why it will never have the mass audiences of football. But what has happened in football, traditionally a working class sport for the past hundred years, is that the game now attracts all classes. Rugby's chances of catching up, despite all the hype, are less likely than ever.

But the main difference is that football, by comparison, is a simple game, easy to watch and understand. It flows all the time, with few interruptions, you can always see the ball, everyone is involved. In rugby, the functions are separate and specialised. A back can be stuck out on the wing all the game, waiting for a pass that never comes.

Halfway through the second-half, by which time England was well ahead, I switched off and raced to Highbury, in time for kick-off. I'll watch England's games again, and hope they get to the final, which the England soccer team will probably never do again in my lifetime. But only if there's absolutely no football available.

On Saturday, at precisely 12.30, I spotted the first gloves of the winter

3 November 2003

FOOTBALL IS A SEASONAL GAME. IT IS PLAYED IN seasons. Inside a football season, there are other seasons, starting roughly at the same time each year, heralding the beginning of, well, whatever seasonal activity is beginning again.

Last Saturday, 25 October, at precisely 12.30, I spotted my first gloves. They were worn by Christophe Dugarry of Birmingham City, the only gloved player on the pitch. A rather fine sighting, much earlier than usual, and made more interesting by the presence of several Africans (Jay Jay Okocha, for example) who have played for most of their lives in hot countries and would in theory be more likely to don gloves, while Dugarry is French, where the winters can be perishing.

I've written to *The Times*, saying I have seen Lobby Lud and I claim my £5. (Lobby Lud was a 1930s *News Chronicle* promotion who went round seaside towns, and if you spotted him—oh, do your own research, or I'll never get on.)

The other hardy annual event, for the sixth time running, is Arsenal being rubbish in Europe. As per usual, they start off with such high hopes, brilliant in England, leading the Premiership, and then come up against some funny foreign teams and—biff, boff—collapse of fragile parties. And each year we get the same head scratchings, followed by the same explanations, trotted out by the clever pundits:

Arsenal are too predictable.

Actually, deep down, they're rubbish.

Hold on, it's the Premiership that's rubbish, not a patch on the Spanish and Italian leagues.

That's the sensible rationale. Then we have the bizarre or the conspiratorial:

Arsène Wenger has a prenuptial deal with Real Madrid to manage them next season, so he has to let them win the European Cup.

Paul Burrell, with all his Diana millions is bribing the Arsenal players to throw games so that shares will go down and, bingo, he can take over the club.

Two seasons ago, it was Wembley's fault. When Arsenal played there, they got stuffed. Now it's clear that Highbury is cursed. Next season, Arsenal will play all home games on Hackney Marshes.

It is indeed a huge mystery, puzzling all Arsenal fans, amusing all others. How come a team who are essentially foreign—Arsenal never have more than three Brits on the pitch and have a foreign manager—get stuffed whenever they play a foreign team?

Wenger is revered in England, but in Europe they know he was a nobody as a player, hardly shining in the Strasbourg under-13s. So they are not scared of him, or his tactics. They also know that Arsenal's defence is porous, like most in England. The top Italian teams have enormous discipline, on and off the pitch.

They take diet and training very seriously, perfecting their skills, obeying tactics and instructions. By comparison, our lads are free spirits, indulging themselves on and off the pitch. Thus Arsenal's defence gives away a soft goal, which leaves Arsenal's attack, so lethal in England, to score, which means it's left to Henry.

Pires is pretty but ornamental. Balls get put over, or threaded through, but there's no one there. Arsenal have no proper centre-forward, someone who naturally gets into the box. Franny Jeffers was a half-hearted and pathetic attempt to solve this problem, but was quickly dumped. I blame Wenger. He's had long enough to sort it out.

I'd have bought James Beattie. I'm sure he'd still be pleased to come from Southampton and improve his England chances. Not a huge natural talent, but he'd play the Alan Shearer/ Malcolm Macdonald role, a worker in the box, always a threat. Until they get such a person, they lack variety in approach and tactics. They might surprise us all against Kiev and suddenly start winning in Europe, but I doubt it.

I fear the seasonal disorder syndromes will continue— i.e., I'll be writing the same column at precisely this time next year.

The crowd was singing: "Missed my drug test and I wanna go home"

10 November 2003

IN THE CAR, ON THE WAY THERE, THEY ALL TOLD ME how well the lads had been doing, what a transformation, now playing as a team, all relaxed, all confident, surely we're going to win something. No, not New Tories, under Old Michael Howard. New Spurs, under Uncle Dave Pleat. Spurs were about to play Boro, my first game in the flesh since the Lake District, and they got me so excited, telling me what I'd missed. Once Hoddle got the chop, a wondrous change had taken place. So they said.

How touching the faith of the average football fan. How their little hearts soar, up to the heavens, off with the fairies, at the merest hint of improvement, such as a small string of games without defeat, or one win on the trot. Sometimes, so I have observed, euphoria can sweep over the most cynical after just ten minutes of their team not giving the ball away.

Inside White Hart Lane, the atmosphere did seem better, more cheerful. Even the grass looked greener, but then English pitches do. They are now rubbish in Italy. Thank God we are better at something. And our refs don't wear those stupid yellow strips.

The last days of Hoddle had been so bitter, so depressing, as we slowly turned against someone once adored. At the beginning of this season, I said to myself: that's it, I'm not renewing my season ticket again, unless they end up higher in the league, I'm so pissed off, year after year, mind-numbing mediocrity. Which was a disgraceful, disloyal thought—how could I have even breathed it to myself? Especially now, all going so well, with a new broom, new heroes to cheer, new chants to learn.

Poss-teega, oh oh oh ohhh
Poss-teega, oh oh oh ohhh
He comes from Portugal
He hates the Arse-en-al

A pinch from Arsenal's Vieira chant but, even so, it was clearly amusing the Paxton Road.

When the ball hits the net
Like a fockin rock-et
It's Zamora

I think that was stolen from Brighton and Hove. There was also a topical song about Rio Ferdinand to the tune of "The Banana Boat Song". "Missed my drug test and I wanna go home…"

I also heard some gossip from a lawyer beside me about the real reason why Rio forgot to take a medical test—and a reference to his sex life which I can't possibly repeat and is totally wrong.

Then came the game itself. Dear God, it was awful. A dreary, goalless draw. In the car going home, there was silence, except for mutterings of sorry, sorry, we was wrong.

Last Saturday, at home to Bolton, Spurs were even worse. Bolton could have had five, as they hit the bar four times. Jay Jay Okocha was brilliant. The fans around me in the west stand did at least give him a clap, showing how decent we are, deep down.

There's something wrong with Robbie Keane. Last season, he was the only Spurs player I looked forward to seeing, hoping for a bit of inspiration and magic, which he did provide. Postiga is a girl's pinny. Zamora is at least trying. Doherty—I have to close my eyes when he's on the ball. I don't think he would make Carlisle's starting line-up.

The only fun bit so far has been half-time in the Boro game. Spurs came out first, forced to wait for Boro to reappear. Because of the delay, the taped music compilation of Spurs songs, which we all know and love, beginning with "McNamara's Band", was going on longer than they had expected, moving on seamlessly into the first bars and the first five words of "Glen Hoddle's blue and white . . .".

The silence was eerie when it was savagely and suddenly cut short, right in the middle of a note. Someone had clearly forgotten instructions from the White Hart Lane politburo that history has been rewritten. Hoddle the manager had never existed, things have now changed.

Oh, if only that were true.

Suddenly, empty seats are appearing at Premiership grounds

17 November 2003

I'M KEEPING A CLOSE EYE ON BLACKBURN ROVERS. for lots of reasons, but one in particular. I like the fact that they were founder members of the league. I like teams called Rovers, so reassuring. Always liked their traditional blue-and-white quartered shirts, not so keen on the modern version.

I look out to see if Matt Jansen is playing, as he comes from Carlisle and has asthma—two excellent reasons to follow him—and also Dwight Yorke, as I did his biog. I follow Souness, whom I first met in 1972, aged 17, in the reserves at Spurs. I gave him a lift home from training as he didn't have a car.

Ten years later, I interviewed him in Italy with Sampdoria. I walked round the block with him and his dog Cuddles, a Yorkshire terrier, and heard him shouting out loud: "Cuddles, come here." In Liverpool, where he'd been the great macho midfielder, Souness would never dare shout out his dog's name. Too embarrassing. See, there are advantages to moving abroad.

Blackburn also make me think of Alfred Wainwright, the great Lakeland walker and writer. He helped found

Blackburn Rovers Supporters Club in the 1930s, acting as treasurer, then chairman. In 1940, he organised the supporters' trip to Wembley for the Cup Final. I suspect part of his passion for Rovers was to get out of the house, as his marriage had failed.

All fans have reasons, some of them trivial, some daft, for following another team's progress. But my main interest in Blackburn at present is in their attendance figures. Last year, they averaged more than 26,000. This year, they are down to 24,000. Not much of a difference, admittedly, but their capacity is 31,367. In recent games on TV, I've noticed rows of empty seats. The club is obviously very worried, exhorting local fans to support the team.

Today in the Premiership we have all-seater stadiums, and the majority of tickets are season tickets. This means that each June we all get conned into paying a fortune for the year ahead, without knowing who the club will buy or sell or how they might do. It is a worrying sign if several hundred fans refuse to turn up for their seats—which they have already paid for. Not to the clubs, as they've had the money and don't give a bugger, but for the season afterwards.

Blackburn has its special problems, because of its geography, so perhaps their drop doesn't mean much. But Leeds's average gate is down by 3,000. Villa's by 1,500. Spurs's by 1,000. These are historically big clubs where you don't expect much fluctuation, unlike clubs that have come up and down, such as Leicester, Fulham and Blackburn.

It's nothing dramatic so far, and a run of good results could see those seats filled again, but I suspect quite a lot of those not going are deliberately throwing their money away—in disgust. It could be the first signs of a virus that might spread to other Premiership clubs.

For ten years now, football has boomed in the Premiership, with almost all season tickets being sold and long waiting lists at the top clubs. Despite the huge debts at many clubs, they have remained smug, self-satisfied, their chief executives paying themselves vast fortunes, telling themselves that at least the fans will always turn up, football will always be popular, forgetting that 20 years ago the game nearly died. In 1986, crowds dropped to 16 million—from 41 million in the post-war years.

This season, I have detected a bitterness, a resentment, among many fans of struggling or poorly performing clubs. Abuse has always been present, but now fans are turning nasty. When your club is doing well, the cost is irrelevant, millionaire players get applauded, flash directors are simply laughed at. But when things start going badly, those are the things that hurt, making fans feel cheated, taken advantage of. Love then turns to hate. Or am I misreading the signs? Hmm. Don't think I'll follow Blackburn any more.

I'd be gutted to die in July, just after I've paid my Sky subscription

1 December 2003

HAD A BIT OF A COLD, FLU ACTUALLY, PROBABLY pneumonia. Well I am a bloke, and my rheumatoid arthritis has been playing up. I was on a drug called sulfasalazine for ten years, which was excellent, then the magic faded. Now started on something called methotrexate, which so far has done bugger all. So, I've been thinking about death.

I've got 12 years or so to go, according to actuarial estimates, which means around the age of 78, I'll be due to pop it. But, of course, they don't say precisely when or how. So annoying. I could make plans, if only I knew. You can decide if and when to conceive, choose the sex of your child, transplant practically every limb and organ, yet when it comes to death, we're in the dark. Before and after.

When our son Jake was about four he asked my wife's mother one day, "Grandma, when are you going to die?" To which Grandma replied, "Soon, I hope."

It would make a great magazine series, asking celebs when and how they want to die, their preferred last words, famous deaths they have admired, oh the scope is endless. I've even got a title—"*Death in the Life Of*". That's a pinch from a series I did begin, when I was on *The Sunday Times* mag.

I've worked out roughly when I would *not* like to go. Not during the football season. I'd be furious to fade away and not know who won the league or the cup that season. So that means some time in June or July. After 11 June, now I think about it, because that's my wedding anniversary. Don't want to let her down. If it happens next year, then please God don't let it be any time in June. I've pencilled in all of June up to the final of the Euro Championships on 4 July.

Looking further ahead, 2006 is going to be awkward as well, what with the next World Cup. Ditto for the years 2008, 2010, 2012, 2014, 2016, 2018. Death at any time in those next 12 years will be bloody inconvenient, what with World Cups and Euro Cups. I think there might just be a window of about three weeks at the end of July. Are you listening, God?

No, hold on. In July, I usually have to pay my Spurs season ticket, which at present is £975, and my half-year season ticket for Arsenal, now £615, and my Sky subscription, which is £30 a month, in advance, twice, because I also have it in Lakeland—then there's pay-per-view at £40 a season, oh my God, I'll be absolutely gutted to go in July, after I've paid all that. And his dying words were, "I leave my subscriptions to arrrggggghh..."

Then again, I might exceed my actuarial lifespan, getting extra points for good behaviour, never smoking, hardly ever drinking, well not more than a bottle of wine a day. Then the methotrexate could kick in and I'll be playing Sunday football again.

I don't find this topic depressing, though I'm partly

saying it out loud, instead of keeping it silent inside, so that by saying it, touch wood, it won't happen. My children think it's awful to talk about death. My wife won't discuss it, but not for that reason. Her motto in life is "Await Events".

It actually cheers me up, thinking of football pleasures still remaining. Three World Cups and four Euro finals, brilliant. During that time I'll probably see three new England managers, Man United and Arsenal reduced to mediocre middle-of-the-tablers, Leeds revived, Spurs winning a game. I've got to hang on long enough to see Bex's next ten hairstyles, Wayne Rooney start shaving, Michael Owen show some facial expressions, Sven caught in bed with another stunner. As for Carlisle United, who knows where they will be. Dead and buried perhaps. It could well be a race between me and CUFC to see who survives the longest.

Yes, so much to look forward to. Gracas ao bom Deus football. I'm working on my Portuguese for next year, so please at least let me live that long. Human beings, nature, life, and football, they all go in seasons. The trick is not to depart in the middle of one.

You could get deep-vein thrombosis from watching too much football

8 December 2003

NEXT WEEK, WE'RE IN EUROPE AGAIN, WHICH MEANS lots of excellent matches, starting at different times, in different places, on different channels. God, I'm exhausted just thinking about it, but terribly excited, of course. This season it's even harder than usual as Sky offers the possibility of watching eight Euro matches at once. How strong do they think our eyes are, how big our brains, how deep our memories? Is it that they think we is an octopus?

I can manage two games at once, no bother, flicking back and forward. I've got a badge for it. A fortnight ago I tried three, following Man United and Chelsea properly, plus Real Madrid spasmodically, just to keep track of Becks's hairdo. What is he playing at? Same style for, oh, must be weeks now.

But it is jolly hard, watching more than one game at once. You really have to be in training. There is a narrative in every game, characters and plot that develop as the play progresses, and which can explain the crowd's reactions and a team's behaviour. Should you flick over to another channel, you can totally miss not just a goal but an injury, an insult, an off-the-ball punch, a mocking kiss, a spiteful spit, a deep sigh, a cynical shrug of a pretty shoulder, a toss of an expensive curl, a sideways glance of deep loathing, each of which, come the denouement in the last act, plus added time, can turn out tremendously significant. Or not.

Watching football these days, especially with back-to-back games, is very much like a long-haul flight. I have often asked the wife for hot towels, more of those little nuts that I don't like, but go on, they're free. OK, I'll have the red wine, as long as it's not chilled, and isn't it about time for the duty-free. I'm sure there will soon be a case of deep-vein thrombosis caused by watching footer, with some idiot having sat in the same position for too long. In fact, my right calf feels a bit funny, stewardess, is there not a masseuse on this flight? I'm going Virgin first class next time.

People brought up watching football only on TV must find it so strange going to a ground. The seats are so narrow, no cushions, only one game at a time to watch, and no one comes down the aisles, along the rows, offering you snacks and titbits. At half-time, it's hellish—everyone rushes at the same time to the same place and the queues and smoke are terrible.

At Spurs the other week, as the queues were so bad, I walked into one of the hospitality suites. A large goon barred my way. Excuse me, my good man, I said. The notice on the door is marked "Hospitality", which in my dictionary means "offering food and drink" and a "friendly welcome to strangers", look it up yourself, Chambers 21st Century Dictionary, page 650. If the notice had said Directors or Players or Sponsors, then naturally I would not have dared venture in there, but hospitality, by definition, means you are offering something free. "Fuck off, right," he replied. Honestly, education in this country has gone to pot.

Europe, in football terms, is an education in itself. It gives us a chance to see how so many of our star players are in fact thugs. They can still be excellent players, like Roy Keane, Steven Gerrard, Alan Shearer, but basically they are hooligans, determined to intimidate the opposition physically. British teams still have a preponderance of heavies, brought up to get the boot in. In Europe, at the top, they have been brought up to control the ball, be comfortable with it, to beat the other player by skill and technique not brute strength. They have that as well, of course. Europeans are just as physically strong and committed as British teams. And they now play at the same frantic pace as we do, even in Italy, where traditionally they built up slowly from defence. I think they've been watching too many Brit games on telly.

I hope to learn a lot this month from all the European games, and enjoy the skill on show, and hope all our lads go through, but I'll also be pleased that this will be the last week of Euro 2004 until February. My calf could do with the rest.

We've seen full-frontal nudity in Scotland, but Wilfred has disappeared

15 December 2003

WHAT DO YOU THINK OF IT SO FAR, THIS HALF-season we have seen? Time for the midterm reports.

Team of the season. Obviously Chelsea. There has never been, in the history of our football, an injection of new money on such a scale. It's worked, so far. But they have to win the Premiership. Otherwise, at every ground next season, they'll be hearing the same chant: "Warrawas-teamoney."

League of the season. The Premiership, of course, because something unusual has happened. At the top, it's a three-horse race, which is good, but Man Utd, Arsenal and Chelsea are so far ahead, even now, that they don't have to look over their shoulders. They are in a league of their own.

We then have a middling league, led by Liverpool and Newcastle, a group of seven clubs who won't be relegated, but won't be in the top three. They are fighting it out, desperately, for the honour and glory of finishing fourth. The third league within the league is the rubbish league: ten clubs, any three of which could well go down. Spurs are ending this half-season as head of the rubbish league. So jolly well done. But I don't expect them to stay there. Too flattering.

Disappointments of the season. Wayne Rooney, alas, has not made such progress as last season. Are fame and wealth distracting him? Is Wayne on the wane? Emile Heskey has been disappointing, but we're used to that. Titus Bramble is beginning to look a total wally. Ronaldo at Man Utd has been revealed as a mere poseur. If he does one more step-over, I'll scream.

Good news of the season. Frank Lampard at Chelsea has grown in the game. Shearer continues to confound those who wrote him off. Scott Parker of Charlton has done good, but I still can't see him in England's midfield. Becks, as a virgin in Spain, has been excellent. But this half-season's winner is Thierry Henry. Arsenal might as well pack up if he gets injured.

Clichés of the season. "Overcooked" has had many outings, all of them unnecessary. All it means is "over-hit". But the winner is Peter Drury. Commentating on an Arsenal game, he came out with the old classic about a player "throwing a right foot at the ball". I hadn't heard it for a while and, for a moment, I was looking down the pitch, trying to see who was missing a foot.

Most puzzlingly pedantic phrase. This was uttered by Barry Davies, when he said: "And even more he." Can you possibly guess what he meant by it? Take it slowly. The context was the Wales-Russia game, where you'll remember that poor old Wales got stuffed and therefore won't be going to

Portugal. Barry had said of one Welsh player: "He came with such hopes." Then he noticed Ryan Giggs and added: "And even more he." See, it did make sense.

Names of the season. My favourite name is XAVI, who plays for Barcelona. When I first saw his shirt, I thought, hmm, is that his name or his number in Latin.

Names you no longer see. Wilfred has disappeared. Wilfreds were at their peak in the 1935–36 season, when 20 of them played in the Football League. I can't think of one in recent years, not since Wilf Rostron of Arsenal and Watford in the 1970s.

Boring sights. Players kissing the club badge on their shirt. So affected. And bizarre. Such as Robbie Fowler kissing his Man City badge. He should be kissing Leeds Utd's. They are still paying him £500,000 a season.

Horror sight. Two weeks ago in the Partick Thistle-Celtic game, there was a scene of total, full-frontal nudity when a Thistle player got his shirt pulled to one side by a Celtic player in such a way that it revealed he was wearing neither underpants nor a jockstrap, thus exposing his full tackle. It did at least prove one of Big Ron's old sayings—it is a man's game.

Chant of the season. In the Southampton-Portsmouth derby, a new event this season, both sets of fans were shouting: "One team in Hampshire, there's only one team in Hampshire." I can't explain why, but it did make me smile. I'm also smiling because I'm off on my summer hols to the West Indies. See you in the New Year. Cheers.

When players make a mistake, Africans don't boo. They just laugh

16 February 2004

DURING THREE WEEKS IN THE WEST INDIES, ALL I caught was ten minutes of a Juventus game in De Reef Beach Bar on Bequia, peering over the heads of about a hundred people, most of them dancing. I knew it was Juve. Like Newcastle United, you can recognise their strip a hundred yards away—on a black-and-white telly, on the blink, through a crowd, on a titchy screen, even after five rum punches.

We had a cottage on that beach, just one room, but elsewhere we were in posh hotels, the Crane in Barbados and the Carlisle Bay in Antigua, both of which turned out to have tellies in the rooms; huge things, flat screens, satellite-connected. I was well made up, well pleased.

"Just you dare turn that thing on," said my dear wife, "Even for one second, and I'm off."

So that was it. The result was that I came home totally ignorant of vital, important, world-shattering events, such as Saha going to Man U, Parker to Chelsea, Reyes to Arsenal, Defoe to Spurs, CUFC winning some games.

Strange, though — while we've been away, no well-known manager has had the push or thrown out his rattle. Usually happens. Usually Kevin Keegan.

I had noticed Reyes's flair while he was at Seville, but it's still a surprise, him being Spanish and that. Can't think of another Spaniard in the works, not Premiership; the Spanish league is so good. But it's also to do with history, geography and culture. The connections with us have never been there, unlike Scandinavia and Africa.

You can see it in the African Cup of Nations, where the leading teams seem to be full of Premiership players, or exes. I'm so pleased to have got back to watch some of the games, though it was hard, what with the jet lag, to work out what BBC3 is and where it was lurking.

African footer is fascinating, such fun, so much to observe. And not just on the pitch. Mark Pougatch, for example, fresh from *Radio 5 Live*. With his specs and well-modulated public-school tones, he looks like Harry Potter's dad. Then Glenn Roeder popped up, proof that he is still alive. And not wearing a suit. Tut tut, Glenn. He was wearing a pullover his mum bought him. Lovely man, so my good friend Gazza tells me, salt of the worsit, but Gawd, does he drone on.

Most African supporters, apart from the Tunisians, don't sing and chant at football, not the way we do, with the same tunes now being heard all over Europe. Perhaps our connections with Africa are all one way. Instead, groups of them bang drums, blow whistles and hooters, laugh and jump about. I noticed this when I was once in Cameroon. When a player made a mistake, they didn't boo, but laughed at him. Must be very hurtful.

The pitches are quite good, the general standard about lower Premiership, sort of Spurs level, i.e., not much cop. The TV pictures come through some French-speaking station, judging by the graphics and subtitles. I love the dancing ball when they give the team formation. So nice to get a different flavour to our TV football coverage.

Best thing of all has been Cameroon's new strip. Couldn't keep my eyes off it. Is it a Babygro or what? The shirt and shorts are all in one, like a cat suit. How do they get it on, when they all have monster thighs and necks? I decided that there must be a zip on the shoulder, so they can climb into it, then zip it up. I bet it's hellish hot inside, and very sweaty, though judging by the number of African players wearing gloves, it probably feels quite parky for equatorial Africans. I was once in Tunisia in March and it was bloody cold, too cold to swim.

I gather the authorities aren't keen on Cameroon's new strip, just as they were against the sleeveless T-shirts they wore a couple of years ago. That was so macho, letting their muscles bulge. This time, with the skin-tight material, their all-in-one gear has looked, well, a bit poofy. Not, of course, that anyone would ever say such a thing to their faces.

I so wanted them to get to the final—and win. Swapping shirts would have been interesting. And very revealing.

Treat triumph and disaster just the same? Spurs fans can't follow Kipling

23 February 2004

THAT'S IT THEN. NO POINT ANY MORE, IN SATURdays, in football, in life, the season is over, nothing now to look forward to. How could Spurs throw away a three-goal lead? And they were good goals, not jammy or own goals, from Ledley King, Robbie Keane and Ziege. Should have given them confidence, ready to come out even stronger in the second half. Perhaps they'd get another three. I was thinking 6–0, 7–0, with Man City down to ten men plus missing Anelka, their most dangerous player.

It's being said they are missing a Dave MacKay figure. They didn't even have a John Pratt figure, someone with guts. Carr is a washout as a captain, who cares if he goes; Dean Richards, what a lump, what a waste of money; as for those geriatrics Poyet and Anderton, bring on the Zimmer frames, let them hobble off, pronto. David Pleat, you are so ugly, and hopeless, wasting our money, my money, but then for 30 years we've had a succession of hopeless managers and spineless teams. Lily Livers rather than Lily Whites.

Against Man U last season, giving away a three-goal lead, that was bad enough, but City are rubbish, even worse than us, with failures like Fowler who were never any good, even in their so-called prime, foreigners who have no idea where they are and care less, plus clueless kids with shaved heads. Just a rabble, really, with no heart, no history of coming back, yet we let them storm back and score four goals to win. In 40 years, I can't remember a worse display. Spurs, you are shite. OK, we won't go down, although I wouldn't bet on it, but we won't get any higher. And we're out of both cups. So it's all pointless from now on. And probably will be. Sans points. For ever.

God, I'm so depressed. Why should I have to put up with this? I don't have to. All pleasure has gone. So I've decided. I'm not going again. You can stuff my season ticket up your arse, Daniel Levy. Not this season, not next. I can't take it. Not any more.

Meanwhile, some time later.

Wow. Life is so good, football such fun. Spurs have scored 11 goals in their last three games, more than anyone, are you listening, Arse-en-al? Those games have produced 20 goals. Amazing. Who says watching Spurs is not entertaining, that you don't get your money's worth? I hate those moaning minnies, threatening not to go again.

Beating Charlton 4–2 away, who are a damned good team, oh yes, plus stuffing Portsmouth and poor old Teddy, ah ha ha, 4–3. That was excellent. Now what was the score in the match before that? Oh yeah, we got three brilliant goals, who could forget them, against now, who was it, City, I think. Anyway, they were real beauties. What a team.

Young Ledley King, future England captain, no question, Dean Richards, a colossus, and Robbie Keane, a legend already, and, of course, with Kanoute and Jermain Defoe we now have three of the best strikers in the Premiership, in Europe, on the planet. And what about Poyet's goal, brilliant, I really think he'll last for ever. And Darren. Class doesn't get old, does it? And please God, Stephen Carr, don't go, we love you, we do.

Now I look at the table, counting on both hands, we have so much still to play for. The way things are working out, with the big gap behind the top three, keep this up, lads, and we could easily make the fourth spot. We could be in Europe. Who knows? The glory days are coming back.

Bloody lucky to be out of the cups. No, think about it. We can concentrate on what really matters. Zooming up the league. This could be our best season for yonks. Can't wait for next. That David Pleat, so dignified, so wise. He knows what he's doing, made some astute buys. And he's quite handsome, in the right light, with the pockmarks in the shade. Beauty spots, that's what they are. We're lucky to have him. Who needs some Eytie manager we can't pronounce?

Gosh, it's so exciting. I feel blessed to have a season ticket. Thank you, Daniel. Come on you Lily Whites.

Football, eh, bloody hell.

I went to Gazza's flat, expecting it to be a dirty lads' den. It was pristine

1 March 2004

I WENT UP ON THE TRAIN TO NEWCASTLE LAST Thursday to see my dear friend Gazza. He has had my manuscript of his life story for six weeks now, but not yet managed to read it. Probably hasn't read a book in his life, that's what you could be thinking. And you'd be wrong. By his bedside, the last time I saw him, were five weighty volumes by American doctors and academics—all about depression and anxiety. But it's true that he doesn't read books for pleasure.

I need talk. I read books for work not pleasure, though they often turn out to be pleasurable. I recently read 50 books on adoption while writing a book about triplets who had been adopted. God, was that heavy going.

Paul met me outside the station, looking great, with a brilliant tan—all from a sun bed—lean and fit with his hair newly dyed silver. Then he started moaning and groaning. He'd got up at two in the morning to start on the manuscript, managing to read for four hours, then he'd gone to the gym. He was now knackered, but had got only halfway through.

I was desperate for him to read it, every word. When he

does the publicity, it would be so embarrassing if he gets asked about things he knows nothing about. I haven't made up any stories, certainly not, but I have put a few thoughts into his mouth that he didn't quite say, though I felt he felt them. I also wanted him to check any facts, dates or names, which I could easily have got wrong and which might hurt other people. I suspect that Roy Keane hardly read Eamon Dunphy's biography of him, not properly, judging by Roy's smirks and evasions when being interviewed.

So I sat with Paul for another four hours while he laboriously went through every page, his head down, his brow furrowed. I said: "Just talk aloud the bits you don't like, I'll make notes, no need for you to write things." But he insisted—correcting all my spelling mistakes. He did, after all, pass CSE English. He failed maths, his best subject, because his desk collapsed. All his fault. He took the screws apart to see how it worked.

While he read, not stopping for food or coffee or even a break (so who says he has an attention deficit problem?), I poked around the flat. He's staying with Jimmy Five Bellies, in his spare room, for reasons explained in the book. Jimmy was out roofing. I hadn't been to the flat before, and half expected a lads' den with fag ends, pin-ups, empty bottles, dirty clothes, dirty dishes. But it was pristine. White carpet, immaculate walls, little glass tables. In the fridge, there was no beer, only Red Bull. Paul, after all, has been teetotal for over a year now. Well done.

After another four hours, he had finished the manuscript, saying he was about to collapse, he could never do that again. But he insisted on driving me back to the station, which I wish he hadn't. I am always scared stiff by his driving.

On the train home, I did have a few drinks to celebrate a successful trip, and got a taxi home from King's Cross. I, too, was knackered, having got up at six to catch the early train. I went straight to bed — little knowing that I had left half of Paul's annotated manuscript in the taxi, the only existing copy.

About an hour later, I was wakened by loud knocking on the front door. I could hear my wife answering it, taking in some package, saying thank you. She didn't, of course, know I had left anything in the taxi, but she gave him a fiver, which was all she had in her purse. It was the second half of the manuscript, about 200 photostatted pages that I'd left behind, but with no title page, neither my name nor Gazza's anywhere. It would have been understandable if the cab driver had just binned it. And I would have been distraught. I don't think Gazza could have read it again.

The taxi driver had driven halfway across London, gone up and down our street knocking at doors, as he hadn't seen which house I had gone into. All for a measly fiver. If you know any drivers of black cabs, pass on the word. I definitely owe him one. There could even be a free copy of the finished book. A thousand thanks, whoever it was.

If fans can be breathalysed at matches, what about those of us at home?

8 March 2004

I'M SO LOOKING FORWARD TO THE EURO 2004 FINALS in Portugal this summer, except I'm worried about the breathalyser tests. Fans will be randomly sampled by the Portuguese authorities and those over the limit will not be allowed into the grounds. The European Commission in Brussels has now decreed that the system will be extended to those watching at home on telly. It would be unfair, so the commission says, just to penalise fans who are in the grounds.

I'll have to be so careful. I can get through a whole bottle of Safeway's Beaujolais during a really tense match. If they raid our front room as I'm slumped there, I could be off, red-carded. The only hope is that we'll be in the Lake District in June. Our house is very remote and my television room is at the back. Surely they won't send random testers that far. Though you never know. Perhaps they'll be disguised as sheep.

Meanwhile, I am so enjoying the Uefa Champions League. All the games have thrown up something of interest, such as the Valencia bench. It consists of dead plush, airline-type seats instead of the bare, hard benches we have in British grounds. Not, of course, that our native managers do a lot of bench sitting. Many stay up in the stands first-half, then come down to rant and rave on the touchline second-half. So they never actually use the bench.

European managers tend to be more sedentary and impassive, though I noticed that the Porto coach, José Mourinho, stood during their whole game with Man Utd, but at an angle, sideways against the dugout, showing no emotion, as if totally bored or spaced out.

Watching Lokomotiv Moscow, I spotted many of their fans with mobile phones, the sort you take photos with, indicating just how wealthy Russians have become. Well, some Russians. The team's shirt sponsor, written on the front, is "Russian Railways", which is apt, because of their background, but also interesting because it's written in English. These top European games get seen around the Continent, if not the globe, so they must be hoping all English-speaking fans will take the train next time they are in Russia.

Real Madrid were dead jammy against Bayern Munich. Beckham looked knackered and I've always thought Raul, the love heart of all Spanish fans, is overrated.

As usual, there have been far too many good games on telly at the same time on different channels, so it's been hellish difficult, either flicking back and forward or trying to set our lousy video machine to work properly. Each morning, I've been rushing downstairs—then screaming and shouting because I've taped some stupid late-night Hollywood film. Next week, I'll be watching a Champions League game in the flesh, going to Highbury for Arsenal's second leg against Celta de Vigo. They can't possibly not win now, after their 3–2 first-leg lead, but like all English teams this season, they can be rubbish at the back.

In Arsenal's case, Sol Campbell, who was never much good at passing the ball anyway, is not at his best and Gilberto is not proving one of Arsène Wenger's greatest buys. I can sense the Arsenal fans turning against Gilberto, thereby ruining his confidence.

As for Man Utd, their whole defence is dodgy. Strange how John O'Shea did so brilliantly last season, got better with every game—and now he's lost it. I think his lack of form is a vital factor, just as much as Rio Ferdinand's absence.

Chelsea, our other big hope, seem to have mucked up their midfield. Last season, their player who had a sudden dramatic improvement was Frank Lampard. But buying Scott Parker, an excellent player in his own right, seems to have cancelled out rather than augmented Lampard's strengths, denying him space, stifling his skills, making him peripheral.

All the same, I expect Arsenal and Chelsea to get through but not Man Utd. It's Fergie's job to sort out that defence, if he can. Has he lost it as well? He's been looking even redder in the face in the past few weeks. Could it be with all the shouting at his team playing so poorly? Or something else? I do hope, for all Man Utd fans, he doesn't get breathalysed on the bench.

Why do footballers need a mid-season break? They have an easy life

15 March 2004

WHAT A SHAME ABOUT HODDLE NOT GETTING THE Southampton job, when you think how well he did managing Spurs, was brilliant running England, so tactful in his handling of Gazza and the others he was forced to chuck out at the very last minute, not his fault, and he did wait almost half an hour to write his account of being England manager, which he had to do, to set the record straight, and he hardly made more than a million from it, then, of course, we have all admired his beliefs, his grammar, so it's a damned disgrace, being so shabbily treated by Southampton when you think, oh I can't keep this up, eeh hee, ha ha ha.

The real point is—it's one of the few examples in football history of fan power. On the whole, we are treated like shit by the clubs, forced to buy rubbish merchandise at inflated prices, £3 programmes full of advertising, tea at £1.40 which tastes horrible, season tickets at £1,000. OK, I take back the word "forced". No one makes us, it's our own stupid fault. But what they do is take shameless advantage of our emotions and loyalty. They know supporting a club is not like having a favourite supermarket. We won't vote with our feet if there are better offers elsewhere. We are lumbered, stuck.

Having shares is a nonsense for ordinary fans, turning up to AGMs a farce. The vast majority of shares are owned by God knows who, companies with strange names in faraway places, controlled by people paying themselves vast salaries as chairmen or chief executives. Their fat salaries upset me most, paid to grind us into the ground financially.

I have this friend, Alasdair Buchan, owner and publisher of *The Diplomat*, who is a Brighton season ticket-holder. Last month—February—they sent him forms to renew for next season. In February! I get livid enough when Spurs do this in June, but I've never heard of a club doing it six months before kick-off. It means supporters are paying ahead for matches they won't see for up to 18 months. When by then the team might well be playing anywhere, with any rubbish players, who might be crocked, banned or in jail if, need I say it, the club itself still exists.

I was just signing a cheque today for an old boys' reunion weekend at my old college in Durham next month—when I read the small print and it said don't pay now, just send the booking form, pay on arrival at the Castle. That's how to treat those whose loyalty and emotion they are depending upon. Season tickets should be similar.

Players' monster salaries don't actually bother me too much. Just the monster arrogance that often results, making some of our British players feel above the law, above normal behaviour, made worse by the craven behaviour of clubs, bending over backwards to tolerate, indulge and defend them.

I was furious that Spurs players were poncing off last week to Dubai, just as I am sure most Leicester fans were livid at the very idea of their dummies swanning off for a hol in La Manga—even before anything went wrong. They have such a soft life anyway, don't have to start work 'til ten, off in the afternoons. Unless they are international players, they have two months off in the summer. Why do they need a mid-season break? For bonding? They are with each other all the time. To have a rest? So they go on a ten-hour flight and stay up 'til five in the morning getting pissed.

It's pure indulgence. And who pays for all this? We do. Directly, through our tickets. Indirectly, through buying crap merchandise and watching on telly.

Our only power up to now, apart from not turning up, which is pretty pointless in the Premiership, as almost all seats have been paid for a year ago, is to boo the players or managers we don't like because they are doing badly. But this happens after they have been signed. The thing about the Hoddle incident is that supporters made their feelings felt and exerted pressure on the board before he could be appointed.

Hurrah for that. After 120 years of professional football, the worms could be turning.

Miles has a contract and a transfer value of £2,000. He's aged eight

22 March 2004

I GO TO THIS CAFÉ CALLED POLLY'S BESIDE HAMPstead Heath most afternoons in the season, i.e., the season when I am in London, walking around Hampstead Heath and going to cafés. Pat, the manageress, is my friend and I tell her about my two granddaughters, they are so advanced, so talented, can draw and act, amazing, and she tells me about her four grandsons who, surprisingly, are equally advanced. One of them, Miles, is very keen on football, so at Christmas I let her have one of my football books, no, not a remaindered one, a new one. I always get excellent service, my cappuccino brought to my table at once, without asking. Now and again she lets me read her Daily Mail. My wife doesn't allow it in our house.

For two years, Pat has been telling me about Miles and his little football teams and I've nodded and smiled, while wanting to get on and read her Mail. Last week, guess what—Miles signed for Chelsea. Aged eight.

Turns out he was spotted by Arsenal when he was six. He'd gone to a little kids' tournament where his elder brother was playing. Miles, being too young, was just messing around behind the goals, kicking about. An Arsenal scout saw him and arranged a trial. He's been training with Arsenal once a week for the past 18 months, getting £4 each time in expenses. It's been very awkward for his mother, Mandy, to drive him there. They live near Heathrow and it used to take her a good hour to get to Arsenal's training ground after school. Several times Miles fell asleep on the way.

They were thrilled when Chelsea came along, as that happens to be Miles's team and their training ground is minutes away. He and his parents went to the very posh Chelsea Village Hotel last week, along with nine other eight-year-olds and their parents, to sign the papers to join Chelsea's academy. No expenses this time, but he does get all his kit and travel by coach from pick-up points to training and games. They play against other academies as far away as Norwich.

He'll go training one night a week and Saturday mornings, plus a match. He can still play for his school, but not his Sunday league team. His parents have been promised a pair of tickets for Chelsea three times a season, while Miles came away with a Chelsea mug and a Chelsea pencil case.

His contract lasts only a year, by which time he could be out, on the scrap heap. If he gets it renewed, year by year, the chances are still hugely stacked against him ever becoming a professional. Might it not affect his school work, then ruin his confidence, his life, if he fails eventually?

"We've thought about that," says Mandy. "But we think he'll get a good training and be in good hands. He has physios and doctors to help and he'll be taught about a healthy diet. At the moment, he does like his McDonald's, like most eight-year-olds.

"But you never know, at 14 he himself might give up. When girls kick in he might lose interest in football training. We've made it clear it's up to him. We'll back him if he wants to carry on, but we're not pushing. Personally, I'm a Spurs fan."

He was told to keep it all quiet until he had actually signed, not go around telling everyone at school. Other kids, and parents, can get jealous. Mandy did worry how Miles's older brother would take it. "He's been fine so far, but we're going to get him to join something else. We're thinking of sea cadets."

One of the things in the agreement is a £2,000 compensation payment to Chelsea if he leaves. That did seem a bit steep, but I suppose he'll have had the benefit of all that training and dietary instruction. But I'd misunderstood. Mandy says the family won't pay it. It's more like a transfer fee: another club would pay it if he gets tempted away by a rival academy. God, it's cut-throat out there.

I would have loved it myself, aged eight, if Carlisle United had asked to sign me, not that children of eight could be signed back then. We were all down the pit, or up chimneys. But would I be pleased today if it happened to my own eight-year-old son? Hmm. Hard one, that.

If you really had to, who would you go out with – Arsène or Fergie?

29 March 2004

FERGIE AND WENGER GO HEAD TO HEAD THIS weekend. No, not kissy, kissy. Headbanging, head butting. Fergie must have been spitting during the week, watching Arsenal and Chelsea still in Europe, while he's been sitting around, throwing things at the cat, eating the furniture. But if he beats Arsenal on Sunday, he'll be all smiles, good fun to be with. So, given the choice, if you really had to, who would you go out with?

Wenger probably isn't much fun on a first date, like going out with the school swot: no small talk, no sweet nothings. You could engage him in some intellectual chat, such as how remarkable it is that three players in his first team have more vowels in their names than consonants — Vieira, Toure and Edu. I bet he'd be impressed. Then you might try to solve one of the great Arsenal mysteries: are those books real, the red ones he sits in front of on Arsenal's pre-match video? Or are they just a phoney prop?

With Fergie, if he's in a good mood and you get on to a second bottle of Fleurie, ask about Becks: did he really hate him so much, or just his wife? What were the Becksy incidents that really pissed him off? Could be gold dust there.

Fergie and Wenger are such different human beings, in looks and personality, yet engaged in the same game. Wenger has edged ahead, without actually winning anything in Europe, but he's doing much better. Under Fergie a good player, such as Veron, got worse, while Wenger turned a good player, such as Henry, into a brilliant one.

Tell Wenger you've noticed how poorly good players have done after they've left his hands, as with Petit, Overmars and Anelka. That's a really subtle sign of good management. Unlike Becks, who blossomed once out of Fergie's clutches.

If a one-night stand with Wenger led to going steady, you would have to put up with TV commentators slobbering all over him, like Peter Drury. "Fantastic, impeccable, immaculate, irresistible, luxuriant, clinical, brilliant, gorgeously gliding." Just some of the Drury drooling over Arsenal's first half against Bolton the other Saturday—a game I was at—which Bolton could easily have drawn. Could you stomach all that for the next ten years?

With Fergie, it's now open season for giving him a good kicking, well deserved, naturally. You could have a useful role in mopping his brow, holding his hand, filling his glass.

Fergie has had ten years of people fawning all over him, so it would be an interesting experience, nobody begging his favours any more, or desperate to keep in with him. Clearly, he expected to retire in his own good time, at the top, ego intact. But events, dear boy, have conspired. He's made some lousy decisions, had some bad luck, such as Ferdinand, and the drug test he missed, and the unexpected has happened in the shape of a moneybags at Chelsea.

When Liverpool had their ten years at the top, some thought it would never end, that this was the world order. Back then, "This is Anfield" would always strike terror into opponents. But it didn't last. Life moved on, pendulums swung.

Man Utd, during their ten years of domination, have had the bonus of enormous wealth, becoming the richest club in the world, even if most of this is from merchandising. It looked as though no other English club could ever compete. But Arsenal have. Arsenal will in turn fade. In ten years, they'll be mediocre, like Liverpool is now, like Man Utd will be next season.

Living with Wenger for the next ten years, would you get any closer to him? Fergie has done endless first-person books, revealed his brutish nature in countless rows. You'd know where you were with him—ready to duck. Wenger has given nothing away. No autobiogs, no public spats, no clues. He's so controlled, so emotionless. Perhaps there's a hidden vice we don't know about, some deep stress behind that cold stare?

Whomever you choose, it's clear how the affair will end. Fergie will get redder and redder—and then explode. Wenger will get more lined in the face, until he ends up looking like W H Auden. Could you put up with that, next to you in bed? It's a hard one. I leave you to decide, pet.

Which of us is off his trolley? Is it David Mellor or is it me?

5 April 2004

THERE WAS AN INTERESTING OBSERVATION LAST week in the *Evening Standard*, a regional paper based in London, by David Mellor, a Tory ex-minister who used to support Fulham, writing about the first leg of the Champions League game between Chelsea and Arsenal: "The pulsating encounter between Chelsea and Arsenal was a good advertisement for the Premiership."

I thought it was dreadful as a spectacle, the two sides cancelling out each other, no one had any space, they were all kicking each other, the passing was appalling and all the way through I was thinking, hmm, if they're watching this in the rest of Europe, I bet they'll be switching off, saying isn't the Premiership shit. And it knows it is. Yet all the fans in Europe chant English. (And sing along to our tunes, such as *Yellow Submarine*. Apple, on behalf of the Beatles, should claim royalties from every TV channel that transmits the sound of any football crowd caught singing it anywhere.)

For ten years, I've kept notes of each game I watch, it

does help me keep awake, in a spiral-bound notebook, 80 pages long, which lasts exactly a season, then I file it away. They're all going to the British Library or Austin, Texas, whichever is quicker on the blower. Very handy in case I forget who scored, who played, what year is it, who am I, what's it all about.

My notes record that Chelsea's goal "was dead jammy, a terrible mistake by the Arsenal goalie" and that Arsenal's goal, a header by Robert Pires, "was the only decent move of the game".

So who is off their trolley, me or Mellor? Next morning, I was discussing the game with the window cleaner, the postman, a drunk at the bus stop, my son the barrister, and a very stupid Arsenal fan I meet most evenings in the newsagent's and try to avoid. All of them said the same: boring, boring.

Only one person that day, a woman called Ali Gunn, a literary agent I happened to be talking to on the phone, said didn't Chelsea play well, they really deserved to win. I said you're wandering, woman, they were both awful.

Then I remembered. She is a Chelsea season ticket-holder. So is Mellor, these days. So you have to know where they are coming from. They were watching it with Chelsea eyes, well pleased with how their lads done—which is to say, they weren't stuffed—and transmogrified this in their blinkered, biased minds into it being a good game. From there they made an enormous leap and imagined it was somehow an excellent reflection of the state of the Premiership. This latter claim is due to brainwashing by television commentators, who have orgasms whenever two

Premiership teams don't give the ball away for longer than ten seconds.

But they are not wrong, those people who thought it was a good game. No critic is ever wrong. Having had 140 books published, I always tell myself when I get a lousy review that it's only their opinion, to which they are well entitled, the bastards.

In football itself, players get very upset by a bad press, but their rationale is to say that because the critic never played pro football, he doesn't know what he's on about. That's satisfying but wrong. If you talk to a player, straight off the pitch, and he is being honest, he knows the score but rarely knows how the game was for the rest of us, its shape, why certain things happened. What he got out of it was a headache, concentrating so hard on his patchwork part.

Last Sunday's game between Arsenal and Man United, another 1–1 draw, was excellent. They were well matched, yet it was an open game, lots of chances, excitement to the end. That's what I thought, me, personally.

One of the joys of football is that even the stupidest person can have a sensible opinion, regardless of age, class, sex, nationality. You don't even have to speak the language. Sign language or chanting "Yellow Submarine" will do. A paradox in football is that we all know nothing, yet we are all experts.

What I know is that whether Chelsea or Arsenal go through, Milan or Real Madrid will stuff them, no question.

If you support an un-successful team, at least the parking's easier

12 April 2004

"ALL YOU SEEM TO DO IS MOAN," SAID MY WIFE when I got home from Spurs last Saturday. "I don't know why you bother going, you get so little pleasure. Why not just watch a game on the television instead?"

"You don't know nothing, woman. You can't beat being there in the flesh, it's what football's all about, innit, always has been, what's for supper."

It was true that going to the match had hung over me all that day, which is daft. I do like Saturday-afternoon games, but it means parking is hellish. It can be a £40 fine on a yellow line. Or being towed away. No wonder local schools are making fortunes at both Arsenal and Spurs, charging £10 to park in the playground.

What a rip-off. That was the cost of a season ticket, not long ago. I refuse to pay. So it means setting off 90 minutes before kick-off, just to find a side street with space, then I have to walk at least a mile to the ground. I'd go by bus, with my free pass, but they're useless.

Once parked, I do like walking with the crowds, communing with my fellow fans, part of the vast body of supporters, all going to matches across the globe. I like to go round the ground, see the stalls, look at the faces, feel the anticipation. Then I love that first glimpse of the brilliant-green grass.

"How funny," said my wife. "That would be the bit I didn't like, mixing with all the other people."

She had been to a gallery and a film, her usual cultural Saturday while I'm at footer. Sometimes she does a theatre, but she prefers a film. She can't suspend disbelief when she's at the theatre, being too aware of the audience, the theatre itself, the actors. At the cinema, she sinks into the dark, feels totally alone, cut off, totally immersed. That's why she likes the cinema best, hence she can't understand why I don't prefer footer on TV.

I explain that being there, you don't just feel the crowd atmosphere, you're also conscious of the players' flesh, the clash of bodies. You can tell who is up for it, who is desperate to win. You take in the whole scene, understand the patterns, watch what's happening off the ball. With TV, you see only what they choose to let you see.

On the other hand, with close-ups, TV makes dodgy decisions clear; goals can be repeated and analysed. At a game, very often you don't see who actually scored: it all happens so quickly. But the emotion is greater when you're there, if it's a goal for your side. Everyone stands up and goes wild. That's really good.

Spurs played well enough—for Spurs. But they got beaten 1–0 by Chelsea, so there wasn't much jumping about. I don't think defeat and the fact that Spurs have a lousy team at the moment are the only reasons for my current state of depression, however.

If they were a brilliant team, winning all the time, there would obviously be more pleasure, but would it be enough to make up for the hell of getting there? Parking would be even worse, if they were a successful team.

I was realising that the misery of going there, which was now hanging over me, was new, resenting having to waste three hours of my life in order to watch a boring 90-minute game. With TV, the game comes to you. No time is lost.

My passion for football is as strong as ever, greater if anything. That's not the problem. Football generally is better, more skilful. But in dark moments, like now, I feel myself wondering if I will renew my Spurs season ticket next season. Maybe just watch them on the box instead.

"Never thought I'd hear you say that," my wife said. "Things must be bad." "It'll pass," I replied. "I'm in a bad mood. Anyway you haven't told me what's for supper."

"It's free play," she said, "remember? On Saturdays, I don't do any cooking..."

Oh God, bloody hell, that's the last straw. What is the point, of life, of anything? Might as well go to bed. Wake me up when it's Real Madrid on Sky.

I can't make out the words of the Euro music except for "Lasagne!"

19 April 2004

I SHOULD HAVE REALISED IT WAS GOING TO BE AN unusual game as soon as I arrived. "Can I look in your bag, sir," grunted a security woman. I have this little black rucksack, so small and bijou you can hardly see it, sort of plasticky, only £2 from a stall in Camden Town. I always carry the same essentials—flask of coffee, orange, chewing gum, petit umbrella. Not once in ten years, taking it to White Hart Lane, Highbury and Brunton Park, has anyone asked me to open it.

"What's going on," I said, half thinking it must be something to do with the game, quarter-final of the Champions League, with Arsenal at home against Chelsea, another London club. Could be expecting crowd trouble.

"Iraq," she grunted. "Thatswotsgoingon."

I do love these European games. I am amused by the words "Uefa Champions League" in all the official literature, without no sign of no apostrophe. So bugger Lynne Truss.

I like the kids standing to attention before kick-off holding little corners of the vast circular football tablecloth, waiting for the secret sign to start shaking it at the billions watching round the globe. I keep waiting for some kid to drop it. I love the Euro music, and yet in all these years, as I sing along, I still don't know the words. All I can make out is "LASAGNE!" which I belt out, ever so lustily.

I want Arsenal to win because my Arsenal friends will be happy. But unlike them, I won't be emotionally distraught if they don't. I want them to carry the flag for English football, progress further, as it will mean I'll have an exciting semi-final to watch against Real Madrid. By good luck, my half of the season ticket I share has included all the top games.

It was true they'd had a nasty shock against Man United, knocked out in the FA Cup semi-final. That was a sickener. But in the Premier League they were still unbeaten. At the previous League game, the programme had included two large features on "the many records created throughout Arsenal's glorious history", which now included the longest unbeaten run in any one season. Boasters. At least Arsène Wenger has not tempted fate this year by predicting they might go a whole season unbeaten.

In the previous two months, I had detected slight signs of slackening. Against Charlton and Bolton, they'd won only 2–1 and in the second halves they were fortunate to hold on. At the time, I'd thought it was overconfidence. Thierry Henry can be too cool, deliberately low-key when he scores and quietly arrogant, which must infuriate the opposition. But after the Man United defeat, I had decided the answer was simpler—Arsenal were knackered.

It's not just fresh bodies you need at this stage, but fresh ideas. Claudio Ranieri, by tinkering all season with

Chelsea's large squad, had fewer tired bodies and tir minds. I also wondered whether it was a devious plot by Roman Abramovich to indicate that Ranieri was for the chop in order to unite the team behind him.

When Wayne Bridge scored Chelsea's winning goal, three minutes from time, a remarkable thing happened. Around me, Arsenal fans left in their thousands. At Spurs, people pile out of the West Stand ten to 15 minutes before the end of every game, regardless of the score, effing and blinding. In 30 years of going to Arsenal, sitting in their West Stand, I have no memory of ever seeing so many leave so early.

It was eerie, at the final whistle, descending the concrete stairs. Total silence, as if they had come from a funeral, heads bowed, minds numb. Usually, people are shrieking and shouting at each other or into their mobiles. I imagined the phones vibrating in their owners' pockets but being ignored, the tragic event just witnessed having dumbed all senses.

What an unexpected result, and how strange the atmosphere, though nothing as weird, I assume, as at Real Madrid and AC Milan. The whole European hierarchy made a nonsense of in just two days. Not that it bothers me, being a football tart. Come on, you Blues.

…lutions to the Becks …em? He becomes …ger of Spurs

26 April 2004

LOTS OF THINGS HAVE BECOME CLEAR THIS SEASON, such as: only three teams have the remotest chance of winning the Premiership, and Carlisle United will need the miracle of all miracles to stay in the Third Division, but there are still far too many mysteries.

Why is Jamie Redknapp captain of Spurs? I suddenly saw him the other week and my first reaction was heh up, what's he doing here. Lost, poor soul, wandered on to the pitch by mistake. Then I remembered that two years ago he had been acquired on a free transfer—far too expensive, but Spurs do throw their money around—and been injured ever since. Spurs is of course a charity, taking in the sick, the lame, the homeless, but why the hell has he been made captain? He has no connection with the club, is not an international, can't play, can't lead. Very mysterious. Does he know something, or is David Pleat in love with him? He has got gorgeous hair. We are told that Rohan Ricketts and Stephane Dalmat no longer appear because Pleat doesn't like them any more. So are Pleat and Redknapp going strong? Photos, please.

How does Brian Marwood find work? As one of Sky's

commentators, he is so wooden that he makes Clive Allen look hyperactive. He tells us what we can already see, repeats every banal remark twice, and spins out sentences by adding "in this football match". We know it's a football match, Brian. That's why we tuned in. Then he goes all schoolmasterly and says "we've talked about that earlier" so we know, dear God, that he's going to repeat himself again—and that's exactly what he does. And if he says "exactly what he does" again, I'll scream.

It must be a plot by the Ron Atkinson fan club. The more that bores like Marwood and Allen appear on the screen, the more we all shout, "Bring on Big Ron." At least his nonsense is amusing.

Who ate all the pies? ... is now clearly totally out of date. The modern version is: "Who drank all the champagne?" Watching Fulham the other day, I noticed a hoarding behind the goals saying "Champagne Lanson—the champagne of Fulham FC". They haven't even got their own ground, yet they are wallowing in bubbly, probably bathe in it, wash their jockstraps in it. Who pays? Is it free? If you know, Fulham season ticket holders, give us a bell. Or a bottle.

Michael Owen, does he smell? He hasn't had a good season, poor poppet, but I've noticed that when he does score a goal, there are few of the monster hugs and passionate kisses his team-mates used to slobber on him. All theories welcome.

What do managers and coaches shout from the touchlines? Often we can read their lips, or body language, but I suspect most of it is total rubbish, which is why players long for the second-half to get out of earshot. I have a suggestion. Why not play the video of a game and get the manager to talk us through the bollocks he was screaming at the time? If he can remember.

When did Steve McManaman start playing with his hands? I couldn't keep my eyes off them while at a Man City game. He's either pointing with them when he's on the ball, indicating where he wants players to move for his cunning pass, or waving his arms at them afterwards for being stupid. Even when he's running around, going nowhere in particular, his arms are flapping like a penguin's. Is it something he picked up with Real Madrid? Should Becks be careful where he puts his hands?

What will Becks do next? That's the numero uno mystery. Will he join Chelsea, as the clever clogs are predicting? I think he will return, once Madrid's manager gets the push. But not to Chelsea. He'll return to the club his family in Essex always supported, where his son is now training, to a team about to have a vacancy for a new captain, only those with gorgeous hair need apply. Yup, look out for his arrival this summer at Spurs. Not just as captain, but joint owner. The present gang are clearly about to sell up and he and Posh have got the money ready. The manager's seat has been deliberately kept empty, waiting for someone tough and determined. Perfect for Posh. And a perfect way to keep an eye on her hubby.

Strange and confusing, the double standards at play on race

3 May 2004

IN THE 1970S, FOOTBALL COACHES WERE REALLY racist. At Spurs, there was one trainer who made jokes about monkeys and bananas, and honestly believed no black player would ever make it in England. They couldn't take the bad weather, the heavy pitches, were muscle-bound but chicken when the going got rough, and were basically Fancy Dans.

Fans could be just as bad. Clyde Best, who played 186 times for West Ham between 1969 and 1975, was about the only black player in the top division for most of those years. He took a lot of abuse. I interviewed him in 1971 and he rather brushed it aside, as if he hadn't heard the taunts.

Thirty years later, I met him again in Bermuda, whence he had returned, and he admitted that it had been far worse than I had imagined. "I got hate letters, abuse on and off the pitch. Players said terrible things to me. All black people—nurses, teachers—had to put up with it at that time. I was on my own, as a footballer. My dad told me to stick it out. He said I owed it to everyone to make a go of it. 'It's not for you,' he used to tell me. 'It's for all the people after you.'"

Those who came afterwards were mainly British-born blacks, well used to the weather, the language, the so-called dressing room banter, and by 1978, with Viv Anderson, we had the first black footballer playing for England. In the 1990s, they were joined by black foreign players, most of them already stars in their own right. Today, in many teams, there is often a majority of black players, native or foreign. In Arsenal's starting team against Spurs last Sunday, seven out of the 11 were black.

I don't think that in ten years I have heard racial abuse at Premiership games, though they say it goes on in the lower leagues. Arsenal fans clearly adore Thierry Henry and Patrick Vieira and appear oblivious of their race. Vieira has become Paddy, just as Robert Pires has become Bobby, showing they are one of us.

All fans now know that blacks come in all types and sizes, all shapes and shades—just like, well, everyone else, thus disproving those 1970s stereotypes. Marcel Desailly is clearly one of nature's aristocrats, in looks and hauteur, and speaks three languages. Thierry Henry is more your professional type, lean and wiry, so clever and smart. I can see him with a wig on in court. Shaun Wright-Phillips, one of our home-grown blacks, is small, thin and weedy, so unlike the dear old images of black players with barrel chests and monster thighs. Carlton Palmer always looked clumsy, physically uncoordinated and ugly. But if you wanted to really scare the bairns, I think Martin Keown, who is white, would do a better job.

Fans are used to the variations, and love or hate players for reasons not connected to their race. It was interesting last Sunday listening to the Spurs fans abusing Sol Campbell, whom they still despise for deserting them. I didn't hear anyone call him a black bastard. Just a common or garden bastard.

Inside the game, they are all brought up together, learn to rely on each other, to kiss and hug, shag the same women, often at the same time, so I can't believe that today any white British player, or manager, has racist tendencies. Even in private. At least that's what I thought, until Ron Atkinson's reference to niggers.

Such an archaic term to use. People have suggested it's his age, 65, and a sheltered, blinkered life, still influenced by those coaches from his youth. He says he didn't know what he was saying, he just blurted it out. Yet as manager of West Brom, he did so much to help the careers of black players. Strange and confusing, the double standards at play when it comes to race.

Shaka Hislop, now goalie at Portsmouth, tells a story of when he played for Newcastle United. He was at a petrol station near St James when some kids aged about 12 started shouting racist abuse. Then one of them suddenly recognised him and shouted, "Hey, it's Shaka." All of them immediately asked for his autograph.

Hislop's initial reaction was amazement, then he walked away without saying a word.

A big welcome to Delia. At last, a woman of substance in the Premiership

10 May 2004

IT'S THE TIME OF THE YEAR WHEN WE SAY IT'S THIS time of the year. So step forward, the season's triumphs and disasters, and if you can keep your head when all about you are trying to read the manager's motto on the dressing room wall, you're a better man than I am, Gunga Din.

Most Successful Team: Arsenal, sans doute.

Most disappointing team of the season: Arsenal, bien sur. So talented, so entertaining, so consistent, yet when it really mattered, they failed. Europe was vital to them, however much they might now rationalise losing it. And they were no nearer to it this season than in previous ones. Football, like life, is pyramid-shaped: the higher up the slopes you get, the fewer remain, but the bigger the disappointment if you fall off.

Newcomer of the Year: Who has come from nowhere, shown great skills off and on the ball, scored when it mattered and run rings round David Beckham? Rebecca Loos.

Newcomer of the Year with the Best Name: Kaka of AC

Milan and Brazil. He's got such skill, and so handsome, but it's his name that endears him to all in our household, as in our house it means poo, shit, wee-wee. "Kaka is on the ball," the commentator just has to shout, and all my children collapse.

Haircut of the year: Not awarded. First time in ten years that no player has won the tonsorial prize. Becks does not count, as he's wearing a retread. Players must show more imagination next season.

Baldie Heed of the Year: Goes to a ref, the Italian Pierluigi Collina, who is making even more money than Ms Loos, now that he's appearing in all those adverts.

Where are they now?: Ron Atkinson, departed, early doors.

Nice phrase of year: "The landing gear is up"—Billy McNeill, describing a player getting ready to dive in an Old Firm game. Also from Scotland, from the Dunfermline manager after they beat Rangers for the first time in more than 30 years: "That gets the monkey off our neck."

New word of the year: "Casterstrophic"—Bobby Robson after Newcastle let in a late goal.

New meanings of the year: "Cynical!" when a foreign player commits a foul. "Honest attempt," when an English player does the same.

Team on the wane?: Man United. Still so many great players, but this could be the season we saw them start to slide.

Supporters of the Year: Carlisle United's. Imagine, 9,524 fans turning up to watch them go down.

Good players with poor seasons: Supposedly at their height, yet they did little—Juan Sebastian Veron, Adrian Mutu and Hernan Crespo of Chelsea; Harry Kewell of Liverpool.

Young players marking time: Wayne Rooney made little progress; José Antonio Reyes flattered but didn't deliver.

Young players who did progress: Shaun Wright-Phillips had a great season. Also Cristiano Ronaldo of Man United, who seemed about to disappear up his own bot with all his tricks, but has started to play simply and sensibly.

Player of the Year: Thierry Henry, of course, but an honourable mention to Alan Shearer. Just when you thought he was over the top, becoming too reliant on backing-in to defenders, he turns in an excellent season and scores some stunning goals.

World Player of the Year: Currently Ronaldinho of Barcelona. Last Sunday against Espanyol, he was the nearest thing on the planet to a footballing genius. Makes Zinedine Zidane look lumpen.

Farewell, my lovelies: Surely we won't see David Pleat again, please God, but I'll miss Claudio Ranieri for his good humour, Eddie Gray for his dignity, and Gerard Houllier for his red scarf and his lips moving as he talks to himself. A big welcome to Delia. At last, a woman of substance in the Premiership.

Things to look forward to: Portugal, of course. I'm off now for four weeks, but will return for Euro '04. I predict that the final will be between Portugal and France. England will get to the semi-finals, then play like kaka, as alas they so often do.

EUROPEAN NATIONS CHAMPIONSHIP 2004

A visit to Lisbon, arise Lord Rooney, it's all turned Greek

I visit Lisbon's Stadium of Light and see a live eagle paraded on a rope

14 June 2004

I HAVEN'T DECIDED YET ABOUT THE ENGLAND POP-up gazebo (Argos catalogue price—£49.99) with the England logo on both sides, which looks excellent, but I have got a set of six England paper napkins and paper tablecloth, only £3 from Wilkinson's, a cheap shop in Carlisle. And I have told my wife that if there's anything she might want to say to me in the next four weeks, then say it now, lass, or hold your wheesht.

But my main preparation for Euro '04 was to go to Portugal, check out where England will play. Half the ten stadiums are brand new, the other half substantially rebuilt. Lisbon's Stadium of Light, where England will meet France on Sunday, and where the final will take place, is new and magnificent, known by the locals as the Cathedral of Light. It was full, 65,000, for Benfica's last match of the season.

I'd tried and failed to get a press seat, the bastards—look, I am from the *New Statesman*, I said, but strangely it didn't work. Big clubs in big cities, like Man United, tend to be so arrogant, dismissive of the press as of the public. So I bought a seat behind the goal, only £20. Lots of space, no need to stand as at Highbury or White Hart Lane when people want out. In front, on the back of the seat ahead, was a holder for drinks. Very handy for England fans. No programme, which they don't do in Portuguese league games. How can they ignore such an easy chance to make money? My little umbrella got confiscated as a security risk. I bought a red Benfica raincoat and ten postcards of Eusebio.

By being so near the touchline, I got a bit of a shock when a live eagle appeared in front of me. It was being paraded around the ground by a bloke who had it on a rope, followed by roughly 30 pubescent dancing girls waving silly plastic whisks. Do they have a name, those sticks beloved of drum majorettes? The eagle is the symbol of Benfica, but I don't think animal rights people in the UK would allow it. The huge crowd cheered the eagle and politely clapped for the girls. In Britain, the girls would have been greeted by lewd leers, raucous whistles and obscenities.

Then I went to Coimbra, where England will play Switzerland. The staff could not have been more helpful. I got a tour of the ground and looked inside the England dressing room. Coimbra is a provincial city, though an ancient one, with one of the oldest universities in Europe, founded circa 1288. The stadium holds just 30,000 but has been hugely renovated at a cost of 50 million euros. It was reopened not with a prestige footer game, but a Rolling Stones concert.

I had to shield my eyes from the multicoloured seats, a mass of clashing blues and oranges, trying to work out the motive. Blue is the colour of the PP, orange the colour of the PSD—the two parties now in Portugal's coalition government. This has pleased the politicians, and might well have helped with all that funding, but the colours were chosen at random by the architect. He just wanted to brighten up the stadium. Ignore any commentators who detect political significance.

Academica, the local team, just managed to avoid relegation on the last day of the season. It would have been embarrassing if they'd gone down on the eve of hosting a major competition, in a municipal stadium on which so much had been spent.

In the square outside the stadium was a road show taking the Uefa Cup in a glass case to all the main cities in Portugal. I queued up with local kids and got one to take my photograph with the cup. I look great, big cheesy smile, but you can't see the cup. Ruined by the reflection from the glass. Or my cheap camera.

Everyone in Coimbra is thrilled they will be the focus of European attention, if just for two games. More than 500 journalists had been to look around already, 400 of them from England.

The Portuguese are a modest, reticent, unpushy people, but they are passionate about football. And they are no longer one of the poorer countries of Europe. It's not just the stadiums that gleam, but the trains and public transport, so much cheaper, more efficient than in the UK. The city centres are clean, bright, welcoming. Let's hope the English fans don't muck it all up.

I open some Mateus Rose at half-time and spot the vicar in an England shirt

21 June 2004

SOMETHING STRANGE HAPPENED DURING THE ENGLAND -France game. Well, a lot did, but I mean here, while sitting in my little TV room in Loweswater. It's my Lakeland library, so I have loads of books around, should any of the 31 games get boring. There's also a little shower and lavatory, so I can have a pee and still watch the footer, which I'm not supposed to do. Jolly handy.

There's another room running off it, which we call the washroom, containing boots, raincoats, deep freeze and washing machine. That's not so handy. I don't know how many times I've told her, but she will walk through my TV room to get stuff out of the freezer, or put on the washing machine, which roars to a climax, shaking the whole house just at a vital moment.

There is a brilliant view from the window, which is behind the TV, but then all our windows have brilliant views of lush fields, wild fells and, behind them, three lakes, three pearls on a string.

I was waiting for the England-France game, checking my vital supplies. I have every free Euro 2004 wall chart published so far, four weeks' supply of crisps, peanuts, and an ironic bottle of Mateus Rose for kick-off. Post-ironic, actually.

Mateus Rose was a joke drink when I was a lad writing the Atticus column on *The Sunday Times*. That was where Mateus Rose was first mentioned in print by one of my predecessors, Sir Sacheverell Sitwell, so he always claimed, saying he was responsible for introducing it to Britain. He was upset he never got a free supply for life.

While looking out of the window, I chanced to see someone walking. They were wearing what looked from the back like a white England shirt. With the walker was a dog. It's Henry, I shouted, jumping up. No, not Thierry Henry. Henry the black Labrador who writes a column in our parish magazine. It must therefore be the vicar—wearing an England shirt. Who says the Church of England is fuddy-duddy. Inger-land, Inger-land.

So I was in a really good mood at kick-off. As were England. Wayne Rooney was remarkable, Ledley King was deadly, Paul Scholes smelled of goals, the whole team was playing good, except Becks, who looked a bit peripheral, a spare tattoo at a biker wedding. They were passing ever so well. Sven's decisions seemed to have paid off. When they got one up, I thought that's it, we'll win now, not just this match, but the European final, the 2006 World Cup final, the play-off against Mars, the whole damn shooting match. Inger-land, Inger-land.

I opened the rose at half-time, which I wasn't going to do until after they'd won. But what the hell, after all those friendly matches where England had been shite and I had been furious with them, now, fair dos, they were showing that they really did have some world-class players, in fact a world-class team, probably win the 2010 World Cup as well. Inger-land.

Now, should I buy some flags for my Jaguar, and a shirt? That was my first thought. Then I thought, could I have imagined it was the vicar, wearing that England shirt? I'd seen it only from behind. It might well just have been plain white.

So I rang the vicarage and spoke to her. Didn't I mention that our vicar is a woman? The Rev Margaret. She was appointed last year and I don't know her very well yet, though we are both on the paper round, taking turns to deliver the daily newspapers in our valley. "Er, was that an England shirt I saw you wearing or did my eyes deceive me?"

"It certainly was," she said. And not ironically either. She is a keen fan, follows Newcastle United and England. She played hockey as a girl, then she was a physiotherapist, so a sporty type. I asked if she had flags on her car as well. "No, I think that would be too much and might scandalise the valley."

So what did she predict, not the Next Life and all that, but the footer? "Oh, France are so strong, if they beat England, they could go all the way." It looks as if she will be right. I went to bed so choked, so depressed after England caved in, but I awoke with a smile, thinking about the vicar in her England shirt.

Ok, so the England team are boring—but that's a fascinating problem

28 June 2004

LYNNE TRUSS'S NEXT BOOK IS GOING TO BE ABOUT football, which is good news, as she was awfully amusing and observant when she wrote those personal pieces on matches for *The Times*. The bad news—wash your mouth out, Lynne, spring-clean your punctilious mind—is that her main point will be that football is essentially boring. How could she think such a thing, during Euro 2004? Is not Wayne Rooney a genius, a saint, a veritable god? Have England not scored more goals than anyone else so far? Leave it out, Lynne.

Or has she got a point? England played boringly against Switzerland for 70 minutes, managing only 20 minutes of reasonable stuff. Against France, they were excellent for 45 minutes, then went back to being rubbish. In the Croatia game, they gave us a fright when the Balkan side got their second goal, but they played well, were positive and composed, and (thanks to the Blessed Rooney) it was an exciting game. It does seem that England have got better as the games have progressed, but no doubt they'll get boring, and infuriating, and useless, and we'll all be clutching our heads and hiding behind the couch again soon.

Sven deserves most of the blame for the boring bits. It's caused mainly by nervousness, lack of confidence, lack of energy and enthusiasm. The only player who is blameless is Lord Rooney of Scouseland. It's Sven's job to fire the team up, not sit around in his suit, folding his arms, buttoning his lip, saying and doing nothing. We don't want sweet reason. We want stupid passion. Sven's style has translated itself on to the pitch, where there is no longer a captain, anywhere, in any position. No shouters, screamers, motivators. Sven did well to stick Rooney in from the beginning, which was a bit of a chance, as the striker hadn't had a brilliant season. So, full points there. His use of Darius Vassell, whom few of the experts have ever rated, has also worked out.

In international competitions, teams are rarely the sum of their parts. France, Italy and Spain have many excellent individual players, world-class figures, and so, to a lesser degree, have England and Portugal. But the problem is to get them to function together, as a unit, as well as they perform for their clubs.

There are obvious reasons why this might not be so easy. Your best national players might all play in similar positions, as with England's midfield, and so cancel each other out. Many star players, such as Thierry Henry, depend on a certain supply, the right environment, to be the focus and focal point. Even first-class players often have to play out of position and take secondary roles in their national teams. A rich club can buy from anywhere to ensure the perfect balance. A national team, even with riches to draw on, has to accommodate what it has. Sven gets more than

£4m a year to solve this problem, and I don't think he's done it. So far.

Most people would agree on his first-team squad. There's no one left at home whom I would have included. So his choice of players is not controversial. It's what he's done with them, or failed to do with them, that's the worry. He has neither moulded them into a unit, imposed or even created a pattern of play for them nor, worst of all, inspired them. David Beckham, Michael Owen, Steven Gerrard, Paul Scholes have all underperformed. Are they poorly, carrying injuries, or just ill in the mind with the worry of it all? Whatever the reasons, Sven is there to sort them out. Only Rooney looks as if he's enjoying it, playing like a free spirit. Somehow, the rest have become inhibited, indecisive, grey and, yes, boring. A bit like Sven himself, or the image he gives to the world.

But this problem is actually fascinating. Admit it, Lynne. How will Sven sort it? Will they all suddenly come good together? I think they will, with St Rooney getting even more goals. Portugal, whom I dearly wanted to do well, will be able to say that at least they got put out by the winners. By the way, Lynne, I've got a suitable title for your footer book: *Shoots, Scores and Leaves.*

Let's get back to proper balls. I didn't like that silver thing at Euro 2004

5 July 2004

WE ALL AGREE: SVEN IS NOT MAGIC, ENGLAND ARE mediocre, Fergie did right to get shot of Beckham. So that's it then, over for another two years, until we go through it all again, same old heartbreaks. Many people probably did give up after England were humiliated, the fly-by-nights, the flag-wavers, thus missing a chance to watch sans stress and experience some new delights.

Such as all the Big Countries of Europe getting shafted. England, Germany, Spain and Italy have the main populations, big leagues, big television audiences, big wads, but each departed, early doors. Four smallish countries, with minor leagues and piddling monies, made it to the semis— the Czech Republic (10.2 million), Greece (10.6 million), Portugal (10.1 million) and Holland (16 million). Each has a population at most a quarter the size of any of the Big Four and, apart from Holland, each is usually seen as economically poor. So, well done to them all. What pleasure it must have given to their peoples.

Some appalling jokes. Gary Lineker's were the oldest: "Let's not mock, Tudor" and "Alan, that's unusual for you to go Dutch".

I also heard "Heinz does give variety", "Czech mate" twice and "Clockwork Orange" three times, but Clive Tyldesley was quite neat pointing out before the Holland-Sweden quarter-final that we were watching oranges and lemons.

Some nice images which will stay with me 'til, oh, at least this evening. They include Luis Figo's fleshy pout, Wayne Rooney's joyful cartwheels, Greece's German manager going hysterical, Beckham's accusing stare at the piece of turf that had deliberately moved — so, of course, the missed penalty wasn't his fault. Will that be the end of Becks? Has the brand reached its sell-by date?

Things I won't miss include John Motson. He is all facts and no insight. Even worse than his empty laughter is his belief that he's become loveable. It's also time we de-pleated our reserves, of David Pleat, I mean. If he says "here we see" again, I will scream. What do you think we're doing in front of the telly, Dave?

Also the ball, that silver thing. I never got used to it. Looked as if it had been kicked over from an Algarve beach. Let's hope we get back to proper balls next season. And I don't just mean Big Ron.

Best fun has been that every single newspaper expert got it wrong. They didn't even predict either of the two finalists, Greece and Portugal. They mostly tipped France, followed by Italy, Spain, England. I've kept their names, and lists, oh yes, and will mock them next time I meet them. (OK, so I woz wrong, 'cos I tipped France to win, but I also said Portugal would do well.)

I did miss the exoticism of the World Cup, seeing players

from far-flung places, different styles of play, facial features, bodies I didn't know from television. Europe has now become homogeneous, familiar, so it was good that Greece did well, introducing us to new names, new players.

Why did England play that last game in black armbands? Was it explained beforehand? Must have missed it. Then again, I read 20 newspapers on D-Day and still don't know what the "d" stands for.

On the whole, apart from England, it's been a huge success. Well organised, good crowds, huge TV audiences in all the countries, even the so-called minor ones. Football is clearly in a healthy state and greatly enjoyed. Unless you supported England …

It also showed, despite what some have said, that national teams still matter. It is true that over the past decade, playing for your club, especially if you play for a Big Club, has become more important, more meaningful than turning out for your country, which is often seen as a bore, a chore, an inconvenience, with some star players hardly bothering to get off their arse, climb down from their wallet and put on their national shirt. But when it's the finals of the world's two major tournaments, managers are still inspired, players try their best, show us the talents we know they have, are their fittest ever, fight to the very end, give us their all, let no one down, unless of course it's England …

OK, I take that back. Let's not finish on a sour note. Chin up, smile bravely, and see you next season.

2004 – 05
SEASON

CUFC hit the Conference,
what does Sven do?
The world's first sponsored
football column

I propose flogging for footballers who take off their socks

6 September 2004

SO FAR, WHAT DO YOU THINK OF IT, THEN? THE season, of course. so much has happened in such a short time.

Two Premiership managers gone already—Paul Sturrock and Bobby Robson, with hardly time to warm the bench, throw a hairdryer across the dressing room, be given a vote of confidence by the board. Getting a million or so in compensation won't make up for the heartache and shame. Poor old Bobby. Just when he thought he was about to retire gracefully, in his own time.

Floods of Spaniards, arriving on every boat, onions round their necks, sorry, that's Frogs, stealing our women, displacing our lads. Who would have thought it just a season ago?

Even more amazing, three roast beefs are now with Real Madrid. Who would have thought it, etc. And Becks has had the same hairstyle for oh, it must be weeks now. Michael Owen looks v nervous. Will he cope or get even more tight-lipped? Or be back at the end of the season?

No new Brit teenage talent sighted so far. Shaun Wright-Phillips was last season's thrill, Wayne Rooney the season before. Where have they gone? In hiding, or smothered by that Spanish wave?

Best signing so far—Paul Dickov to Blackburn. A bargain at £150,000. Most disappointing signing—Patrick Kluivert at Newcastle.

Paul Scholes retiring from England duties signified one thing: he is pissed off by Sven and his England management. At his age, his stage, would he have fallen out of love with playing for England if the team had been happy and successful?

The Premiership refs have got their act together at last—commercially. Don't you love those twee little advertisements on their dinky sleeves for Fly Emirates. They are now looking for sponsors to appear on every yellow card. Double price for red cards.

But boo to the new electronic, computer-driven advertising hoardings round Old Trafford. So annoying, distracting, now that they can move around. As bad as watching Spanish football. At least we've been spared the sight of a moving car appearing to appear in the penalty area at a vital moment.

A new advert, not one of the all-singing, all-dancing ones, says: "Budweiser—official beer of the Premier League." Official? You mean there are some unofficial, unauthorised beers going around throwing themselves down the throats of our stout lads? (Not Spaniards, need I say. They drink garlic.)

Refs can now yellow-card you for removing your shirt, and I should think so, disgusting habit, where will it end. I suggest flogging if you take your socks off, imprisonment for lowering your shorts and hanging if you remove your jockstrap.

Rooney: he's given us the best fun so far, not just his transfer saga, but his patronage of certain Liverpool brothels. Wasn't it considerate of him to sign autographs for the prostitutes, some old enough to be his gran. So thoughtful. Shows how well brung-up he is. I'm sure if he'd been a bank robber, he'd have posed for a picture opportunity with the manager before leaving.

Welcome to some nice names. Joonas Kolkka of Crystal Palace—a world first for our football ... Well, I can't think of another Prem player with three Ks in his name. Also to another Palace player, Fitz Hall—known to his teammates as Onesize, gerrit.

Our beloved commentators have returned, bang on form, coming out with some newly minted pearls. "The games come thick and fast at this stage," said Martin Tyler in the first week, which is bollocks. The fixture list schedules the same number of Premiership games every week, throughout the season. If anything, it's at the end of the season, not the beginning, that they pile up, with postponements, replays, cup ties.

But his colleague Andy Gray came out with something that no one could argue with: "We're talking about the player we're talking about."

Hold on, can you mint pearls? Who's talking bollocks now? Yup, we're now well into another new, fun-filled season.

I'm in with the quality at Carlisle United, the Man U of the Conference League

13 September 2004

LAST WEEKEND, I WENT TO SEE MANCHESTER United—sitting in the directors' box, of course, I'm in with all the quality—the Manchester United of the Conference league: the one and only Carlisle United. I watch them in the first couple of months of every season, while we are still in Lakeland, but now, for the first time since 1928, they are not in the Football League.

But a surprising thing has happened. They have sold 1,500 season tickets—compared with 1,400 for the previous season. The gate for their first home game, against, hold on, I've got their name somewhere, didn't even know they had a team, I thought it was a mudflat in the Thames, yes, it was Canvey Island—and yet 7,234 people turned up. Amazing. Better than most clubs in the Second and First Divisions. For their second home game, against Farnborough, the gate was 5,505. They won that game 7–0. The last time they did that was more than 50 years ago, against Rochdale in 1953.

After that, CUFC had a brief spell in the very top division, blink and you missed it. Exactly 30 years ago, Carlisle were leading the First Division, having beaten Chelsea,

Boro and Spurs. Their fall has been mighty, but their fame endures, hence their new status as the Man Utd of the Conf.

You must get some antagonism, I said to Lord Clark (formerly David Clark, MP and cabinet minister), one of Carlisle's directors. All the other Conference clubs will hate you, muttering here comes the moneybags, the toffs, let's duff them up."Oh no, they love us," he said. "We bring enormous numbers of supporters with us, so all their gates are going up."

Away to Halifax, 1,400 of the 2,696 crowd were from Carlisle, while at Forest Green, wherever that is, half of the 1,074 home gate were Carlisle supporters.

"On the other hand, they do all raise their game, as if they really were meeting Manchester United."

For their new life in the Conference, Carlisle have acquired a new owner, Fred Storey, a very big local builder. So big that, when I shook his hand, I still couldn't see his head. Must be 6ft 7ins. He's a local, born and bred, as is the manager, Paul Simpson. I'm trying to think, now that Bobby Robson has had the push at Newcastle, of other clubs where both the owner and manager are locals. Hmm, can't.

One problem for Carlisle is that they still have some players on Football League salaries, up to £1,500 a week, whereas in the Conference, where many are part-time anyway, the norm is nearer £400 a week. And by dropping down, they have lost the £230,000-a-year share-out they got as a Football League club. This season, it's been halved and next season, if they are still in the Conference, it will disappear.

Last Saturday, they got picked by Sky for their live game. How exciting, you might think, for a little rural club, to be on national TV. Ah, but Sky insisted the game should be at midday, not three o'clock, as nature and the fixture list had intended. It was a last-minute change, thus mucking up arrangements for far-flung fans, such as me, 30 miles away, out in the country, and also for those who were working on Saturday morning. The fee from Sky was only £5,000—so a drop in the gate could well make the presence of the TV cameras a nonsense.

It looked a pretty decent crowd at kick-off, though I was busy admiring two innovations since I had last been at Brunton Park. There's now an electronic scoreboard—the wonders of science. I do hope those blokes who used to carry boards with the half-time scores around the ground are being well cared for. And there were drum majorettes who waved their blue-and-white whisks and screamed lustily.

Alas, the game was a scoreless draw—pretty boring, apart from the fun of watching Nigel Clough, Burton Albion's player-manager, send a pass on to the roof of the main stand. We all enjoyed that. The crowd turned out to be 4,582 in total, about 1,000 fewer than the average home gate. So Sky's money did not make up for the lost gate revenue. It doesn't always pay to be the glam club.

Sven should fax in the team sheet, then watch at home like the rest of us

20 September 2004

I SOMETIMES WONDER WHY SVEN BOTHERS TO GO TO England games. He clearly has no role, nothing to do, a spare Swede at a veggie gathering. His staff won't even sit beside him, judging by several glimpses of him at the Poland match, where he was on the bench all on his own, both seats either side empty. Poor sod, I thought, he's run out of *Big Issues* to sell.

Presumably he does wander into the dressing room at half-time, looks around in a daze, offers a few banalities that are either ignored or have the reverse effect, as England usually do worse in the second-half. Then, towards the end, when things get tough, he becomes transfixed, unable to stand up, far less shout, swear, jump about and punch the air, the way it shows you in all football management manuals.

Before and afterwards, he's awfully nice to them, so Gary Neville has told us, loving and caring for them, listening to their moans, soothing egos, giving in to their whims, holding their hands, wiping their bums—which is a useful role, do not mock, all players need that sort of attention. On the other hand, they already have people who perform that function: their mums.

So what is the point of Sven? England have been so jammy, landed in the cushiest group, yet Sven is going to put us through agonies over the next, how long, I have the fixture list somewhere, oh no, we have a whole year to go, until October 2005, before England are safely into the 2006 World Cup finals.

Of course, England will qualify. Of course, Sven will keep his job. We know all that. What we don't know is what Sven does. The main attractions of his job are the money and the women, excellent motivating forces, whether in politics or pop music, while the football is obviously a bit of a chore. For the next two years, he should stay at home. Send in a fax with the team sheet, then watch it at home on the telly with the rest of us.

I sometimes wonder why players bother to turn up. For internationals, it's optional—if you can't be arsed, you say no—but for League games, they have to make some sort of appearance. Yet once a Premier player reaches his twenties, he's a multimillionaire, with all the women he can eat, all the houses he can sleep with, no need to work for the rest of his life. So how rotten, how beastly it must be for him to have nasty managers and coaches screaming at him all day, sometimes being forced to play in a position he doesn't fancy. Then there are fans booing, the press putting in the boot—all so unfair, they just don't understand the pressures, the sleepless nights, the bags under the eyes that make them look 42 not 22, how can they go clubbing like that? Or, in the case of John Terry, 62.

Honestly, I don't know why more of them don't pack it

in at 23, stay at home, count the Ferraris. You have to admire them for sticking it out.

I sometimes wonder why I bother going to games. It takes four hours out of your life, in the flesh, when you can have it wall-to-wall on the box from your sofa in less than two hours. This season, Sky has got even more live games. That's not to mention pay-per-view, which of course I have, Bravo, which I'm still looking for, I don't think it reaches Lakeland unless it's a sheep station, and Sultana, which I think is an Irish channel, plus ITV2 and ITV3 and, of course, basic BBC, all of them now boasting live footer. Last week, on Sky ordinaire, you could watch eight live Euro games in one evening.

What I call my evening lasts from 8pm to 9.59pm, when we run up the stairs, at the double, to catch the peep, peep, peep for The World Tonight on Radio 4. Then we fall asleep, sometimes before the third peep. So that's a two-hour evening. To watch eight live games, getting them on video to view them one after the other—for you can't save them up, can you, there's an avalanche tomorrow—you need evenings lasting not two hours, but 16 hours. Dear God.

I sometimes wonder why I bother living for football. I'm at one with Sven and the players. Really, it's all so exhausting.

I believe (deep breath) that football has become a homo-erotic culture

27 September 2004

YOU DON'T GET MANY FOOTBALLERS WHO ARE poofters, to use the cheap, slangy, dressing-room terminology, which of course I do, even when I'm talking to myself. They would get drummed out, humiliated and exposed very early in their careers, unless they could conceal or sublimate their feelings and inclinations. Which some must do, by the law of averages.

The violently macho posturing of their language and attitudes is often rather suspicious, and might even be a sign of something being suppressed. For I believe (deep breath) that football has become a homo-erotic culture.

From the earliest age, they are exposed to naked male flesh, all day long. Blokes really do preen, prance around, showing off their tackle. They are used to their bodies being massaged and pummelled by other males. You don't get female physios inside dressing rooms. They go out on the piss together. Picking up some tart at the end of the night is an optional extra on a par with a curry or a kebab.

Many of them do treat women badly, having been brought up in an all-male environment. But what's surprising is the new habit of group sex, with them all taking turns, in the same hotel room. It would suggest that watching each other is part of the fun.

However, at the same time, their feminine side has become more open and pronounced, thanks to players like Becks. An obsession with their hair is a modern passion. Before the Second World War, they certainly copied each other's hairstyles, such as a middle parting; post-war, they liked to look like Billy Wright, with waves on top. But then they stuck to it for life: none of this faffing around and changing the colour, ribbons or extensions every damn game. Kissing and cuddling? None of that business went on before the war. A stiff handshake with the person who had passed the ball, then you walked back to the centre circle, tight-lipped.

Today, their natural reaction on scoring, while they await the kisses and cuddles, is to take their shirt off. This is now banned, but you still see them starting to do it involuntarily, pulling it partly over their head or at least up a few inches, exposing a bit of flesh. Why do they do this, o wise one? Because naked cuddles are nicer than shirted cuddles. Physical contact has now progressed even further, with players getting into little huddles, arms around each other, cuddling up, before the game has even started.

Football itself has become more feminine. Look at the physique of the average player. In the past, they were smaller, squatter, heavier—bull-like. Now they are taller and thinner, more akin to ballet dancers than labourers. They wear slippers, not boots, and the rules now protect them from thugs and nasty people who push them into the net.

Perhaps it's all just a matter of Brits generally being more open now about their feelings. Gazza became famous for his tears, but he is also greatly loved by all his friends. I was driving with him and his dear friend Jimmy Gardner, aka Five Bellies. We were on our way to a match at Telford, where Gazza was about to play for Wolves Reserves, when we got totally lost. Jimmy was driving and Gazza was giving directions, as he thought he knew where the ground was, but this was a fantasy. They were effing and blinding and screaming and shouting, blaming one another. Any outsider might have thought blood was about to be spilled, but it was harmless invective, a way of letting off steam. I know what they're like, I thought. They're an old married couple. They appear to be arguing, but in reality it's a form of affection. Lads today, eh?

I'm not suggesting there's anything between them, as I don't want to get thumped, but they are each other's best friend. When Gazza's marriage finally collapsed, he turned to Jimmy for help, going to live with him. You know where you are with your mates. It's how players are brought up today—on permanent bonding sessions.

You won't believe the number of players I hate for their silly hair

4 October 2004

I HAVE A PUNCHABLE FACE; I ALSO LOOK LIKE ONE of those people who drive slowly down the middle of the motorway—according to a letter I got last week. Strange, isn't it, what people hold against you? For about ten years I wrote a column in *Punch* where I referred to my wife as the Old Trout. Silly, juvenile, dunno why I did it for so long, just as I dunno why I use the word "dunno" when I know it's very annoying. Every week, I would get an abusive letter, saying it demeaned not just my wife, but all women.

My wife is getting irate letters these days herself. She's written a book about the diary of a woman, which readers love; but when they get to the end and realise it's fiction, there are always two or three every week who grow furious, feeling they've been cheated (though it does say clearly on the cover that it's a novel). Some even say that they'll never read her books again.

There's not a lot of logic, or sense, or fairness, to these sorts of dislikes, but we all have them. You wouldn't believe the number of players I hate for their silly hair or silly voices. In fact, it's part of the entertainment they provide. We pay a fortune to watch them, making them millionaires, thus entitling us to have no qualms about rubbishing them. "If you can't take the shit, then don't perform in public, be a politician, write or act for money," as my old granny used to say (no, not the one who says she knows Wayne Rooney, the other one).

Currently, here's who I dislike, mostly for potty, petty reasons, which means I might change my opinion completely, perhaps by the end of this piece.

Only two months ago I loved José Mourinho: what a breath of fresh hair; did wonders at Porto; so cool to stand sideways to the dugout, as if oblivious to his team. Now I just wish he'd shave his stupid face, and stop chewing gum and blaming teams he can't beat (such as Spurs) for being defensive. If he's so clever, as he's told us, why can't he be clever enough to see how silly that was?

Alex Ferguson: well, he's a bully, we all know that—all the millions like me who have never met him. Andy Cole: I hate the fact he says he's now "Andrew Cole". What a poseur. And he always has a moany look. I don't like Robbie Fowler's face, or Trevor Francis's voice. Roy Keane: nasty piece of work, you just have to look at that sickening half-smile when he trots out. And David Beckham: I've gone right off him; he's so petty when he gets beaten or makes a mistake, lashing out like a spoilt child. I now believe that in the years when his free-kicks were magic, half of them were lucky, judging by the way nowadays he can't kick straight. Sven-Goran Eriksson: don't get me started. I have only to see his impassive face on the bench to start foaming at the mouth.

Currently top of my likes list, kissy-kissy all round, is

Sam Allardyce. I adore his name, his accent, his big burly unglamorous frame, his little earpiece during games, his obsession with background scientists and experts; so endearing, so sweet, even if it's all cobblers and it'll be out just as soon as things go wrong. Arsène Wenger: not just for being by far the best manager, but for how he conducts himself. When it comes to cleverness, Mourinho is still in the backward class.

Cristiano Ronaldo—who cannot thrill to his play, and also how he plays, never surly or nasty or cynical? At the same time, I also like Robbie Savage. I enjoy his rage, his wrong sort of hair for his character, his stupidity when he loses it, thinking: "Oh goody, something really awful is going to happen." As long as he's not doing it to one of my team, in which case I boo him, like any other normal, half-witted fan.

James Beattie: I am amused he's become a gay icon, so I now watch him carefully—to see the attraction—and yes, he is a bit of a rural hunk; he'd make an attractive farm-hand or sailor. Les Ferdinand: I do like his face (so regular) and his manners.

Rooney: so glad he's reappeared. I like his ugliness, his pasty face, his lack of self-obsession (such a relief from Becks), and his lack of respect for senior players. Now he *has* got a punchable face. Come on, you can see the marks.

Wayne Rooney, unlike Michael Owen, does not suffer from humility

11 October 2004

IS WAYNE ROONEY A GENIUS? CAN ANY FOOTBALLER be a genius? Whatever happened to Michael Owen? Was he a genius? There are just so many difficult questions around at the moment. Why do footballers never dye their hair black? Now that is a hard one. I won't even try to explain it.

After one game for Man United, Rooney was hailed as the greatest Man U player in the history of civilisation as we know it—civilisation as we used to know it, looking back to players we never saw, games we weren't at, times we never experienced, but still confident enough to compare like with unlike and say: "Arise, Sir Wayne, a verie parfait knight." Apart, of course, from his horrible complexion, crap hair and disappearing eyes. And that he did nothing in his second game.

While the media have been ape-shitting, the real experts have been advising caution. Fergie, his manager, talks about Rooney's potential, about what might be "when Wayne gets over the adolescent development". Sensible Uncle Arsène predicts that Rooney will be at his best at 25, 26, and then he should really be something. Me, I think this is obvious, boring, not to mention cobblers. I say bugger the future: let it take care of itself. A phenomenon is here and with us. The chances are that the best is NOW, for the simple reason that, although he might get more pots, he won't get better.

All walks of life, all activities, throw up geniuses from time to time, even in areas of life not always rated by virtually everyone else. I've met loads, from Lennon and McCartney to Alfred Wainwright. Now he was unique. Just look at his seven Pictorial Guides to the Lakeland Fells. Who else would have thought of doing them that way, entirely in his own hand, as fresh today as when the first book appeared 50 years ago?

Rooney has arrived fully formed at 18, the finished article. He can do everything in football, put his own boots on with either hand, wipe his bum while heading, pull on his own shirt, though in that first game he found it difficult. Did you notice that rip at the collar? I thought it was a fashion statement, a throwback to the 1930s, when shirts were laced up at the front. Next day in Cockermouth Main Street, everyone was talking about it. Ron, who sells me football memorabilia, said he knew for a fact that Rooney had split his shirt when putting it on—because his head is too big. Got good contacts, my friends in Cockermouth.

Rooney's incredible self-belief is a mark of his genius. Geniuses tend to have it, though the formula doesn't work the other way. Think of the prats you know who are convinced of their own genius. Rooney retains the arrogance of youth, which is not surprising. He was hailed as a boy wonder while still in nappies and, so far, nothing has gone wrong: everyone still tells him he's brilliant, so how could he not be confident? But more than that, he is a cocky little bastard.

And this is where he differs from Michael Owen. Little Michael was equally amazing at 18; three years later, he scored those wonderful goals against Germany. He was a free spirit; nothing seemed to trouble him—but, looking back, flicking through my mental video, I now see that Owen was confident rather than cocky. A big difference. Confidence can be dented. During his non-scoring spells at Liverpool, and for England, you could sense the nerves, the stiffening of the muscles during the fluffed chances. Deep down, Owen has doubts.

Rooney, on the other hand, does not suffer from humility. His ego, like his body, appears intact, bullet-proof. Clearly, he can't yet be compared with the greats of the past—or even the present. He has done nothing, won nothing, has hardly started his career. And aesthetically, he will never compare with Pelé, George Best or Thierry Henry.

Perhaps he won't even have a career. Injury, loss of form, drink, drugs, gambling, women, too much easy money, too much fame, his big head, a nasty manager or plain boredom might well ruin his potential. We can all predict what he might win one day, but as a player, playing for our enjoyment and his own, this is his peak. Naturally, we all hope that Rooney will stay at that peak, but at 18 going on 19, he is as good as he'll ever get. Enjoy.

Hunter Davies writes his first ever sponsored football column—and looks forward to many more deals

18 October 2004

EVERYTHING IN FOOTBALL NOW HAS A SPONSOR, from monster new stadiums and the sleeves on football referees' shirts to—I can announce today, with pride and pleasure—the world's very first sponsored football column. From now on, it will be called "The Eddie Stobart Fan". Or THE EDDIE STOBART FAN. Perhaps even E*D@D?I&E!. Graphic designers will be working on the new logo, once they have finished shredding all note-paper and signposting saying "Highbury". Emirates Airlines is paying £100m to have its name on Arsenal's new stadium for the next 15 years. The transport company Eddie Stobart Ltd is paying only £9.99 per season to have its name on this column, but, hey, it's a trendsetter. Built into the contract are bonuses for increased readership, numbers of letters to the editor printed and, if I do well in Europe, any columns that get syndicated.

I've already taken delivery of my sponsored motor, bearing the famous Eddie Stobart livery. At the moment, parking is fine, as we are still in the Lake District and there is a very large field right beside our house. This is empty at the moment, as the Herdwick sheep are being sold at Cockermouth market.

Next week, when we return to London, it could be awkward. If I do manage to park it outside my front door, that will mean ten houses on either side will be in darkness. Have you seen the size of these 12-wheeled articulated trucks with a trailer behind? Awesome. You can play five-a-sides inside, unseen, no bother. I plan to ring both Spurs and Arsenal on my return, in case they are holding any secret trials for new players and don't want the paparazzi from the *Camden New Journal* to find out.

Mine is called Coleen. All Eddie Stobart trucks have women's names. It's named after Wayne Rooney's girlfriend. On her return from her spend, spend, spend spree in New York on her pre-pre-pre-Christmas shopping trip, she wanted to put a little back into society. It is, of course, thanks to the modern-day sponsors, fighting each other to have every inch of football flesh and football-related objects covered in their name, that Wayne was able to become a millionaire while still aged seven, playing for Our Lady of Goodison primary school's first team.

Ah, such a sweet, romantic piece of football history, soon to disappear for ever, just like Bolton's Burnden Park (now Reebok Stadium); Stoke City's Victoria Ground (Britannia Stadium); Bradford City's Valley Parade (the Bradford & Bingley Stadium); and Leicester City's Filbert Street (Walkers Stadium). When Everton eventually move, their spanking new ground will be called the Granny-a-go-go Massage Parlour Stadium. That was the highest offer they could get, poor sods, but they're not exactly high-profile any more, now Wayne's departed.

I do have to wear the Eddie Stobart company tie and uniform while typing, and for the photo shoots for the in-house magazine, when I get to pose with Ffion. In 1998, when it looked as if William Hague might become our Great Leader, his fragrant wife had an Eddie Stobart truck named after her. William himself turned up to do the unveiling, of the, er, truck. I'm not sure if I'll have to pose with Ffion or her truck. The latter is a bit of a shed these days, but the former has quite a few thousand miles on her, especially now that her literary hubby has a fresh vroom in his piston.

Hold on. That's Eddie himself on the phone from Carlisle. He's just heard the latest news. The Bradford & Bingley Stadium and the McAlpine Stadium have each had another name change. They plastered their logos all over the shop, made us all get used to saying their silly names, mucked up all the programme notes and football results, and really really annoyed James Alexander Gordon, but now they are off. I dunno. That's sponsors for you.

Eddie now thinks he'd prefer to sponsor one of the stadiums up for grabs, instead of a potty little footer column. I can keep the tie, but he wants the truck back. Right, anyone—your name here for £9.98? OK, 10p. Right, I'll accept washers.

In Cockermouth, you don't get the same quality of fantasy as in London

25 October 2004

BACK TO LONDON, AFTER FIVE MONTHS IN LAKE-land. So many scary people. Where do they all come from? The bad tempers; the filth and litter. Something has always gone wrong in the house that I didn't expect. This time I couldn't get Sky, despite my paying them a fortune. A wonky "scart lead", whatever that is. Then my photocopier broke. Rang Staples (used them for years) and ordered one. In their catalogue, they promise next-day delivery. Still waiting, six days later. They'd even run out of copy paper. What is going on?

No booze in the house, so spent a day on the phone to Safeway's, Chalk Farm. Failed to get through to the wine department; all human life departed. Left order on switch-board, for 48 bottles of Beaujolais. That should keep us going until Christmas, or next month—perhaps next week, the way my children knock it back. Went on Saturday morning to pick my order up, and they had no idea what I was on about. Got stared at as if I were an alien.

In Cockermouth everything works: the shops are help-ful; services are great; only the sheep are scary. London is shit. No, really, what a dump. Why do we come back?

What has it got that Lakeland hasn't?

And so to Arsenal. Last Saturday, they happened to be at home, and my half-season ticket to be kicking in for my first Premiership game of the season. Not a huge treat, as I am well used to watching unbeaten teams. (Oh yes, have you seen Carlisle United's position in the Conference?)

I was even offered a second ticket for Arsenal, by my friend the judge. His son had decided not to go, as he is fed up with people around him moaning. Unbeaten in 48 games, and they're moaning.

On the way there, me with three Arsenal fans, they were saying that the away support had been down this season. Several games had big gaps at the clock end, where the visitors usually scream their heads off. (Must be the seat prices: £33 for the cheapest.) Is the football world becoming sated with Arsenal's seemingly endless success? One said that he wished the run was over: the tension was killing him.

Walking to the ground, I saw this crowd gaping through a hole in the fence. My wife, when she sees gapers, or any accident or incident, crosses the road, looking resolutely the other way. I immediately rushed to gape. God, it was amazing. In just five months, an architectural wonder had sprung up: white bridges leading to a giant-and-beanstalk creation that soared into the sky, all loops and waves, as magnificent as Lisbon's Stadium of Light. Through the gaps, fans were taking pics with their digis.

I wished I'd had mine with me. I do have one, and a mobile phone and a computer, none of which I've used in a year; but I do have them, so no one can say that I'm out of touch. What I wanted to take was a Lowry-type shot of the massed ranks of fans pouring down Avenell Road towards Highbury's old East Stand, that historic listed building, part of the fabric and history of English football. The building itself is being retained, but such a crowd shot won't be seen in the future.

Aston Villa scored first, which was just as well, as Arsenal kept their mettle — no fannying around — and proceeded to be, well, rather wonderful. I even jumped up twice, which I had vowed not to do out of loyalty to Spurs. A fair score would have been 8–1, not 3–1. At times, Arsenal were mesmerising.

Arsenal programmes are £3, compared with £2.50 last season. Tea and coffee prices have gone up. The club now has fashionably flat TV screens in the corridors showing footer — something Spurs have had for years. The two teams shaking hands before the kick-off is new to the Premiership, but they must be having a laugh before kicking each other. Sylvain Wiltord doesn't get moaned at any more. He's gorn. That's about it, facts-wise. I do like to keep a record of these things.

Forget the facts, though. What I experienced was fantasy — the way Arsenal played, the look of that futuristic stadium. You don't quite get that in Cockermouth. Nor even in Carlisle, where CUFC got beaten by Barnet in front of 9,215 people. OK, I admit it. Some things are better in London.

It's social progress when autobiographies of footballers are in hardback

1 November 2004

AT LAST, WHAT A RELIEF, 'GAZZA: MY STORY' IS OUT of the bestseller lists. For the past 15 weeks, he's been in the top ten in *The Sunday Times* non-fiction hardback list, beating piddling people who have done little in their lives, such as the former American president Bill Clinton, whose autobiography came out on the same day. Gazza's did twice as well. So far, 250,000 copies of his story have been shifted. Appalling, of course, what the world has come to.

But it's part of a modern trend. Fergie, Roy Keane, Beckham—their autobiogs all topped the hardback list, which usually has been dominated by literary or political figures, as it should be, come on, we do usually have standards. They are clearly being lowered. Just look at all the space in our newspapers devoted to stupid old football, whole sections, acres every day, compared with the poor old book reviews, which you can hardly find these days, even in the broadsheets. Disgusting, where will it end, etc. Will that do, dear? I'm just trying to keep her happy. She goes on all the time about the football coverage taking space and attention away from proper books.

I've tried to tell her. Football biogs and autobiogs have a long and interesting history. For a start, you didn't get them back in the 1880s, when football became professional. Publishers just didn't consider the lives of horny-handed, working-class professionals worthy of notice. Football books did exist, of course, right from the beginning, but they were written by, about and for the posh amateur gents and their amateur clubs. Very soon, however, the popular press began to devote space to match results and our heroes, but they still didn't make it on to the pages of hardback books.

Footer biogs and autobiogs began in the 1930s. Probably the earliest, in the form we now recognise, was Herbert Chapman's autobiog in 1934. I'm still looking for a copy, but in my football library—more than 500 books so far—I've got George Allison's *The Inside Story of Football*, from 1938. A cheap paperback, it was published by Quaker Oats, complete with a competition for free gifts. By the look of it, he wrote it himself, but then he had been a journalist, before becoming Arsenal's manager.

After the Second World War, the autobiogs came flooding out. Usually in hardback, but pretty thin, 150 pages or so, nothing controversial. Not written by the star player himself, though they pretended it was. Mostly it was done by a football hack on the local paper who got a few hours with our hero, then cobbled it together from the cuttings. Much like many today, really.

One of my most treasured books is a first edition, with pristine cover, of the first ever autobiog by Stanley

Matthews. *Feet First* was published in 1948 by Ewen & Dale, a firm long forgotten. There is no credit or clue to who actually wrote it. "I intended to start this book in 1939," it begins. Stan, at that time, was just 23, already a star. His father told him not to. "Who do you think you are—Fanny Walden?"

I've also got Eddie Hapgood's 1945 autobiog, *Football Ambassador*, and *Football From the Goalmouth* by Frank Swift (1948), each "edited by Roy Peskett", so it says. Presumably Peskett did the actual writing. I keep them in plastic, along with Len Shackleton's famous 1955 autobiog, *Crown Prince of Soccer*. It's famous because of Chapter Nine, which is entitled "The Average Director's Knowledge of Football". The chapter is totally blank. Before I secured a copy, I thought this was legend rather than fact. (It's actually just one page blank—page 78—but amusing all the same, for 1955.)

A lot of early stars from the First World War and the 1920s, such as Billy Meredith and Hughie Gallacher, never got their biogs written until modern times. Publishers now realise that footer biogs do sell, not just those about Becks and Gazza, but of stars long gone.

Anyway, Gazza is my last soccer autobiog. I'm now doing a non-football life. He's Scottish, knighted, lives in the Bahamas. Here's another clue: he was once offered a trial by Man United. Before a three-hour session, we warm up by discussing football. See, pet, my football reading has not been wasted.

With all the football on TV, some fans won't bother to go out for live games

8 November 2004

SOMETHING STRANGE WOKE ME FROM MY REVERIE. Not that I was reverie-ing, just lightly dozing. Trying to watch eight matches a night for three nights is not easy. You think I just sit there, slumped? Oh no, it's exhausting, working out what's going on, who's playing, is Christmas over yet, who is the Prime Minister.

Usually I rely on someone like Brian Marwood to keep me from totally nodding off. When he says for the tenth time "in this football match", I manage to stir myself. "Brian, we know it's a football match. That's why we switched on." Or Andy Gray going on about "this greasy pitch". "They been pouring chip fat on it then, Andy?" I yell back at him. "Someone's used too much hair gel, eh?" Pitches can't be greasy, Andy, not when it's just rain on grass. "Slippery" is the word you want, son.

All the advertisements around the grounds also help keep me awake and wondering. "Duck and Cover", for example. Is it a pub, an insurance firm, an instant meal? And "Rainham Steel". I didn't know they made steel in Rainham, but if so, do they expect people at football matches suddenly to think: "Hmm, at half-time, I won't have a pie, I'll order a couple of tonnes of steel instead?"

Then I realised what had awakened me. All the empty spaces. I've noticed this already at Highbury this season, gaps at the away end, even in Premiership games, though just a few, not enough to register on the Richter scale. (Remember him? One of Harry's dodgier signings at West Ham.) But when it comes to Carling Cup games, and many of the European ones, at home and away, we are now seeing vast empty spaces.

Do the seats cost too much? I don't think that's the reason. At most Premiership clubs, the early cup games are often included in the season ticket you have already bought. So you are not paying extra money. Unless you are an away supporter.

Are we then perhaps overdosing on footer? There are so many live games on television, either all at the same time, leaving us to choose, or one after the other, such as all day and evening on Saturday and Sunday. Some fans can't quite be arsed to get up out of their seats, or leave the pub, to drag themselves to the actual game.

On Saturday, for example, there were two live games on Sky for which I had paid extra, because they were on Prem Plus. I must be mad. In fact, I've paid twice. At our Lakeland home, I paid £50 for the season, back in July. I tried to switch it when we got back to London, but not only would Sky not let me, they charged me £75 for a new subscription for what's left of the season—i.e., a much bigger sum, for a lot fewer games. Bastards. Don't get me started.

Anyway, the timing of these two games, which now appears normal practice, was 12.45pm and 5.15pm. If you want to see a game live, and fortunately there are a lot more Saturday three o'clock kick-offs this season, which is what nature intended, you can't see the two TV games, not properly. I managed only the first half of the 12.45 game on telly before leaving for Arsenal. Even rushing back, I missed the first half of the second game. Yet I've paid for all three, and wanted to watch all three.

The timings are so stupid, working against those who want to support their local team. There must be many fans who are beginning to think fuck it, I'll stay at home.

The first football game seen on television was in 1936 between Arsenal and Everton. It was filmed, and shown later. In 1938, the then FA Cup final was shown, but only part of it. From the 1950s, the FA Cup final was shown live, every year, oh the excitement, taking your seat on the sofa, hoping to see the wives in their best frocks and beehives. Regular weekly football on TV began in 1964, with Match of the Day screening highlights on Saturday evenings. Since 1992, and the creation of the Premiership, we have had a whole TV company, Sky, whose marketing is based on having exclusive live football.

During these 68 years, almost on the hour, it was said that television would ruin gates. Seemed logical, but it never did. Could it now be about to happen?

"You called me a bastard," said the voice. "Last week in your column."

15 November 2004

I WAS JUST OPENING A RATHER EXCITING-LOOKING package from Arsenal, with a drawing of the new Emirates Stadium on the front, ooh, gorgeous, when the phone rang.

"I'm one of the bastards," said a voice.

Wrong number, I said, and if not, I don't want double glazing, don't care if I've won a prize, and haven't you anything else to do in Delhi on a November afternoon than bother me about mobile phones when I don't even use the one I have?

"You called me a bastard," said the voice. "Last week in your column."

Course I didn't. I don't use such language, and if I did, er, you're not a lawyer, are you?

"No, I'm your friend from Sky TV..."

Oh, one of those bastards—sorry, I mean, one of those awfully nice people—at Sky, one I do happen to know, who helps bring us all those excellent football games.

"That's what I wanted to talk to you about," he said, and continued to natter on for more than half an hour. He told me that Sky gets uninformed fans like me going on all the time about how it has been changing the kick-off times just to suit itself. Which is not true, so he said. There can be a variety of reasons for tinkering with kick-off times, oh yes, often to do with the police, or other games, and anyway it's all agreed with the Premier League.

And if gates at League games do go down because of all the football on TV, which is what *The Observer* might be telling its readers, Sky for one would be very sad. Oh yes. It wants happy faces on the terraces, and no spaces. That helps the atmosphere, and pleases everyone, naturally. Sky doesn't like being associated with events nobody goes to.

If gates for cup games do go down, think what a good challenge this is for the marketing men. It gives an opportunity to reduce prices, let in kids for free with their dads, make special concessions, which an excellent club like Charlton have done, when they see a less-than-full house coming up.

I thanked him for making it clear that any nasty things being said because of Sky were not true, and if they were, they were nice things. I think I got that straight. Possibly. In passing, he did come out with some interesting statistics. Guess how many live games Sky showed in the first season of the Premiership, 1992–93? The answer is 101. And today, in the 2004–05 season? A total of 500, if you include the 50 pay-per-view games. I wish I'd had those facts last week when I was moaning on, sorry, being grateful for all the TV footer. When you add on the number of games shown by the BBC, ITV1, ITV2 and Channel 5, the total is now more than 750 matches per season.

"Yet so far, more people are watching Premiership live games on Sky than at this stage last year. And don't forget, last season, total attendance in all five divisions was the best for 35 years. If you suggest otherwise, I happen to be a Spurs fan and I know where you sit..."

Perhaps he didn't say that last bit, but by then I was at last tearing open the exciting-looking Arsenal envelope. I still have my half-season ticket for Arsenal, paying a friend £634 while his son is working abroad, but I've been following the progress of the new stadium. It will be almost twice as big as the old one, so there's bound to be a lot more seats available. Might be cheaper as well, as Emirates has paid Arsenal £100m.

Very glossy, yummy brochure, lovely big photos, then very small print saying that only 6,500 people out of the 26,000 on the waiting list will get ordinary seats. So hurry, hurry now and buy what they are calling Club Level seats. These don't look all that great to me (I prefer to be much higher), yet a halfway-line seat will cost—wait for it—£4,750 a season. You have to take it for four years, paying half the money up front—yet the stadium doesn't open until August 2006. You do get free drinks at half-time. Big deal.

Bastards, bastards. And no, I won't be answering the phone next week.

A day with the hacks. Top breakfast, plush seats, but not a player in sight

22 November 2004

MUST BE ABOUT TEN YEARS SINCE I WAS IN A PRESS box but the other week was Spurs-Arsenal, bound to be a punch-up, so I wanted to be close to the action. If any. Every reporter I talked to beforehand was predicting a boring 0–0 or 1–1 draw. They are experts.

When I used to do match reporting the press facilities were primitive but, if you stood in the car park long enough, you could grab the odd player. Now, with all the agents, attention, not much chance, but at least the hacks get treated as fairly civilised animals. So we got a hearty English breakfast, yum yum, in the press lounge beforehand. It was a mid-day kick-off.

In the old days, you had to fight for a team sheet, which was often chalked on a board. Now you get all the details, properly printed, plus pages of totally fascinating facts, such as if Robert Pires plays and if he scores he will be three short of 50 Premiership goals: wow, hold the back page. If Spurs keep a clean shirt, their laundry bill will be well down next week.

Normally, at Spurs and Arsenal, I'm in a season ticket seat, high up, just over the halfway line, excellent position, can see every move. The press seats at White Hart Lane are, in fact, rubbish, as far as academic analytical study is concerned, which, of course, is my speciality. Too low down. You can't see what's happening on the other side.

But you can see everything happening on the bench, right in front of you. I could read what Chris Hughton was writing—just squiggles really. Pat Rice, on the Arsenal bench, whom I studied closely, has lost about three inches since he used to play for them. Weird. Arsène Wenger sat down throughout, except when he got up and kicked a crate of Lucozade, ooh, the bad-tempered beast, after José Reyes missed a sitter. Martin Jol, in his first game as Spurs head coach, never sat down. In breaks of play, he looked up at the West Stand, as if trying to catch a friend's eye. Or God's.

Jamie Redknapp, Spurs captain, one of my pet hates, why is he still there, sat on the bench throughout, thank goodness, so I had lots of time to peer into his left ear and examine his tan. All over, even his hands. He went out of his way to shake hands with Thierry Henry, chatted to Dermot Gallagher, the fourth official. Even had his arm round him. At one stage, he turned round and gave me such a lovely smile. Now I understand why he's still there. His role is to charm for Spurs.

Afterwards, all the press traipsed into the interview room, which was like a Soho viewing cinema, 60 very plush, luxury seats. With Bill Nicholson, you tried to pin him against a wall and force two sentences out of him. Wenger appeared, sat on a dais before us, answered all questions, fluently and intelligently. He made only one grammatical mistake, one all Brits make, when he said Arsenal has "less tall men". His pronunciation of "comfort-able" was quaintly French and he said "cuh-shun" not "coo-shun" for cushion.

Martin Jol kept us waiting, but he was equally expansive, another foreigner with excellent English, though I got a bit lost when he said his players had been "like birds flapping". I was impressed by what he said, even though he must have been pretty choked to lose 4–5. Yes, turned out far from boring.

There were 70 hacks in the press box—I nicked a copy of their names, the sort of trivia I treasure—including star reporters from the nationals, such as Patrick Collins from the *Mail on Sunday*. He said all managers do turn up, except Fergie. Chelsea's press box is worse, being low and in a corner. It was Ken Bates's final revenge on the press.

There were reporters from France, Holland, Sweden and Norway. I sat beside Sindre Olsen from Aftenposten, in London to report Norway-Australia later in the week. He had bombarded the Spurs press officer John Fennelly and managed to get a seat. He loved the food, the comfy chairs, was impressed by all the press facilities—except access to the players. In Norway, he gets into the dressing room after every game, even while some are still in the showers.

Ah, those were the days. In England's case, that was last allowed in about 1863, the first year the FA was formed.

That player who has old, worn eyes. Didn't Baden Powell warn him?

29 November 2004

THERE ARE THREE AREAS STILL HIDDEN FROM US BUT otherwise we are living in privileged times, we football fans, seeing and appreciating and understanding more about our heroes than our forefathers ever did. And it grows better, all the time.

I am sure each weekend that if every Premiership player, which means almost 300, were to walk straight out of my TV set into my living-room I would recognise them at once, be able to say: hey, that was a terrible miss from the free kick, who were you supposed to be marking at that corner, I saw the handball the ref never saw, don't lie, that cut over your left eyebrow, not as bad as I thought, I do like your new boots, shame about the colour, but your tash is coming on great. Our forebears were never privy to such knowledge and particulars.

Jonathan Greening, for example, of West Brom. I've been watching him carefully all season and can state categorically that he has a beard, making him the only beardy in the Premiership. David James of Man City may indeed be acquiring one, of a sort, but we all know, we intimates, that he is a creature of fashion, so it might not last.

Harry Redknapp of Portsmouth, poor lad, his facial twitches grow worse. I do feel sorry for him, exposed to us all as he stands on the touch line. He must know that TV close-ups are now so close, so cruel. Lee Hendrie of Villa, we all wonder how a man so young can have such old, worn, eyes. What does he get up to at home? Didn't Baden Powell warn him? Igor Biscan of Liverpool, he does make me smile. Close-up, he always appears half asleep: Stan Laurel's love child, who by chance has stumbled out of bed and into Anfield.

We who were watching the shambles against Spain knew in minutes that Rooney had lost it: his eyes told us, his body language was clear and brutal, yet it took Sven, who was there, somewhere, 40 minutes to haul him off.

With Ronaldinho of Barcelona—there are around 30 from the Spanish league who I feel equally on first-name terms with—I am studying his gob, staring right down his throat. I now think his apparent smile, so charming and delightful, might simply be caused by his teeth being too large for his mouth.

The team at Juventus are also my personal friends. I now witness their most intimate moments, such as how before kick-off they kiss each other, on the cheeks, sometimes the lips. Oooh. But alongside the human ticks and mannerisms, the game itself is what we now see best of all, can understand goals and misses and failures that were a mystery to us in the past.

What we don't see—and probably never will—is, first, inside the dressing-room. Wouldn't that be wonderful, to be there before, during and after the match, hear the coaches, feel the tea cups flying? I would love to observe the final team talk, to understand what it was they thought they were supposed to do.

Second, we never see training. I'm sure it would be possible, as long as not too many secrets were given away. It could provide a fascinating insight, be so informative, letting us see footballers' real working lives, their day-to-day exertions, not just their weekly 90 minutes.

The third area could easily be shown, as it's not hidden away. I would like Sky's cameras to linger longer on players who have been subbed and are now on the bench. Small moments, but so strange. It was being at Spurs the other week, sitting just a few feet behind the bench, that reminded me how weird players are when taken off, disembodied, unable to speak, focus, even see properly. They have been concentrating so hard, so tensely, that being suddenly removed totally disorientates them. A steam, a glow, surrounds their bodies, making them ethereal. It points up what has been happening out there, on the battlefield, the state of unbeing they have been in. Very revealing, yet so hard to describe in words.

Oh well, I suspect it would come over dreadfully boring. Not even the wonders of modern TV can capture three dimensions and four senses. Not yet anyway. But smellies and feelies should be with us soon.

I thought I'd solved the parking problem, but I ended up fuming again

6 December 2004

THAT'S IT, I'M SORTED; THE REST OF MY LIFE, HOWever long or short, is now organised. All I have to do is get up each day, make it to the weekend, and, most important of all, stay alive. Something that has driven me mad for two decades is over. So I thought.

I have this friend, an architect with a young family, who went up to Old Trafford from London to cheer on Arsenal. Safe enough outing, as we all know the vast majority of Man Utd fans are well-behaved middle-classers living in Kent. He enjoyed the day, despite having to spend nine hours on the train. Nine hours! I couldn't believe it. Nine minutes and I'm frothing.

I've gone through life unable to wait. I see a queue, a one-way sign, a "wait here" signal, and I think, "Hmm, doesn't apply to me, it's for other folks", so I either ignore it or turn around.

So getting to football these days, either at Spurs or Arsenal, is increasingly pissing me off, having to go earlier and earlier in order to park. Public transport round here is useless. When I was a lad, there were no cars, no need for them in caves. In big cities, there were special buses laid on to take you to the game. Why don't they do that today? Or park and ride?

My posh Jaguar—well, not so posh now, as it's eight years old—is riddled with bashes and bumps with parking in stupid places. I'm not car proud. I just want to get there and back, sharpish. For the past five years, I've done car sharing, taking my turn with other fans. But the new and hellish parking restrictions have made it virtually impossible. You can pay £10 to park in a schoolyard, but they get full an hour before kick-off. Or find some dodgy kid in a baseball cap and hood who says he'll look after it for a fiver, then worry you'll never see the wheels again.

It really has depressed me, hanging over me each match day, taking the edge off my pleasures. Yes, I know it's pathetic. The whole family has said to me, often enough, oh diddums, is that the worst you have to worry about?

Then I had this brainwave. At both Arsenal and Spurs, there's this line-up of Rolls-Royces and Bentleys purring outside after every game, the uniformed chauffeur with the engine on, cocktail cabinet warming up, waiting for some fat bastard who probably doesn't know the offside trap from a prawn sandwich. I bet it's a company car, which he shouldn't be using. I wonder if the shareholders know? Hope someone gives it a good kicking.

What if I hired a modest minicab, a regular order, to take me there and back to every game? Couldn't cost much when shared. I rang round the local firms. Four said get lost, no chance, we don't do no football games. A new firm said, fine, no problem. They wanted my address, which I know, got it written in the front of my diary, and also the pick-up address. I hadn't thought that through. They needed it now, as it probably wouldn't be the same driver each way. I said Drayton Park railway station. I've noticed it's closed on match days, with lots of space outside.

I invited two of my Arsenal friends, this is on me squire, Hunt's treat, and one turned up with his daughter, home from Newcastle University. We left at 2.15pm, which was brilliant, about 45 minutes later than normal, so more time to have a proper lunch, a few drinks, watch the footer on Sky Plus. And it cost only £6. In future, we'll share. Miles cheaper than parking. Afterwards, we all raced to the pick-up point, thinking hurrah, home in time to watch the 5.15pm Sky game. No sign of the minicab. Instead, there was a monster line-up of West Brom supporters' coaches, with the police moving cars on.

I had my mobile phone with me, first time I've used it in a year, and got the minicab firm. The daft driver had gone right on to Highbury and was now stuck in traffic, unable to move. I arranged another rendezvous. He didn't turn up, or we missed him. We all had to walk home, which took two hours, what with the hanging around. God, was I spitting. The man who doesn't wait. And I'd let down my friends, and the daughter, after being so flash.

Well, that's it. The rest of my football-going life is obviously going to be much the same. Only worse.

If you throw yourself around, you can make yourself big—and world class!

13 December 2004

ANOTHER WORLD-CLASS COLUMN, FROM A WORLD-class writer, in a world-class mag. Looking out of the window, it seems a world-class morning; I'll just finish my bowl of world-class muesli and go and have a world-class poo, hopefully.

The use of the phrase "world class" this season has become well, world class, but all it means is "not bad", "half decent". A goalie makes a world-class save from a world-class striker. In other words, they are playing in the Premiership, which we all believe, by definition, is the envy of the watching world, and thus far, in this game, they have not fallen over or been subbed.

You never hear a commentator talk about a world-class throw-in, which in theory should happen, what with all these world-class players we are so fortunate to have among us.

"Watch how he opened his body." No, we're not into self-mutilation or anatomy. That's another popular phrase that must be very confusing for beginners. It refers to some big lump of a defender who's closed his eyes, thrown himself into a tackle and hoped for the best.

Equally worrying, if you had just arrived from Mars, is a player who's "made himself big". This does not have sexual undertones, or suggest size-enhancing steroids. It is usually applied to a goalie who has thrown himself blindly at an attacking player.

"A six-pointer" does not appear to make sense, not for anyone who looks at the rules and sees that the most you can get from a league game is three points for a win. Six points is an abstract concept. Don't let it worry you. The thinking is that if you take the three points from a team roughly level with you, while adding three to your own total, therefore opening up a bigger gap, that's twice as good. One of the mathematical mysteries in football is the loss of a point, which disappeared for ever when the change was made from two points for a win. The notional points at stake are now three—but if it's a draw, teams get only one each. Ergo, one point vanishes. Where does it go? I've looked everywhere.

All my long-legged life, I've been collecting football words and phrases, for my own amusement. Now someone has beaten me to a book about them. Two blokes, in fact—John Leigh and David Woodhouse, who started collecting choice footer speak when they were doing doctoral theses in 18th-century literature at Cambridge. One is now a don. The other works in the City. Their book is called *Football Lexicon* and is prettily published this month by the very high-class, literary firm of Faber & Faber. Just shows you, eh? I saw you, scoffing at me for making stupid remarks about world class. There's money in stupid remarks.

Leigh and Woodhouse have compiled a dictionary that explains 800 well-used football words and phrases. These range from "altercation — a euphemistic way of describing a dust-up or bust-up" (as in "bit of an altercation off the ball there") to "Row Z — a long way from the pitch and so, by inference, the hypothetical destination of any no-nonsense clearance".

It's very amusing, clever, not to say spot on, but I would have liked them to have used their academic training to have dug out the origins of well-known phrases. "Custodian", as in custodian of the net, referring to a goalie, is about a hundred years old, but who first coined it? When did it become archaic?

You don't hear of "tanner-ball players" these days, which I was led to believe referred to a player who could turn on a tanner, i.e., a sixpence. I couldn't find "sick as a parrot" in their book, either, yet this is still current and must be about the best-known, most parodied football cliché. But who first said it, or first wrote it, which surely must be something that can be found out? And was there ever a parrot?

All half-decent English-language books will give you etymological origins and early usages, so I wish the authors had attempted more of that, as I'm sure they are aiming at a world-class football dictionary. Hmm. I wonder if "world-class" originally referred to players or countries that played in World Cup finals? If so, which World Cup? There must be a PhD in this.

For the first time in ages, non-fashionable hair has become fashionable

1 January 2005

HALFWAY THROUGH THE SEASON, MORE OR LESS, SO time to take stock, look ahead, and see what the rest of it might bring for all those concerned.

Referee Graham Poll is probably dreading it. I first heard the chant during a Man City *v* Man United game during which he gave some dodgy decisions against the home side. "Oh, Graham Poll, you're a fucking arse'ole," so 10,000 voices sang. Now it follows him around the Premiership. Poor lad, what can he do? He could say that where he comes from, Poll is pronounced "Paul", so sorry, chaps, you're well out of line, rhyme-wise. That might stop them. Or not.

Harry Kewell, he must do better, and also Wayne Rooney. No, he's not done bad, he's just not done good enough. Watch his first touch; he lost a bit of confidence, which is something I never expected. Stewart Downing of Boro, all the commentators have fallen in love with him, but I'm not convinced. Only got a left peg. But I do like the look of young Reto Ziegler, the Swiss blond at Spurs.

Names to savour, because they are new to me this season and, well, they are really, really lovely names. Willo Flood of Man City, isn't that romantic-sounding? Dexter Blackstock of Southampton, straight out of Thomas Hardy; Wagner Love of CSKA Moscow—should be in Hollywood.

There's one chant we may never hear again after this season, but I'm so fond of it. It always makes me smile. "One team in Hampshire, there's only one team in Hampshire." Sung by both Portsmouth and Southampton fans. Most fans north of Watford probably never realised there was even one club in Hants.

And banners, well, let's hope we get some good ones. Best one so far was held up by Sporting Lisbon fans at Newcastle's St James's Park, and was written in English: "Thank you for the lovely night out, Newcastle Girls." Wasn't that sweet. Or was it satirical?

Managers, don't say we'll lose any more. So far, there have been new ones at Blackburn, Newcastle, Spurs, Southampton, Portsmouth and West Brom. Who will be next to go? Keegan at Man City, Chris Coleman at Fulham?

Hair: nothing much to report this season. Fashion-wise, for the first time in ages, non-fashionable hair has become fashionable. I'm thinking of people who haven't changed their hairstyle since primary school, when their mum did it for them, such as Lee Hendrie, Mark Delaney, Gavin McCann, all of Villa. Who copied whom? "Oooh," one of them must have said in the dressing room, "you look cool." Paul Scholes of Man U has of course always been a trend-setter when it comes to crap hair.

Let's hope we don't copy the latest fashions for refs in

Italy. Have you seen their new frocks? Fluorescent lime-green matching top, shorts, sox. Ugh, I have to avert my eyes.

Will Everton disappear in a puff of blue smoke, slowly slithering down to their normal, boring position so that we'll forget they were ever up there, with the Gods? I hope not. It would be nice to see them give Chelsea a run for their money, money, money.

I don't believe for one moment that José Mourinho had his fingers crossed for Barcelona. It was a double bluff. Which he is. A walking, talking, posing one. But his supreme self-confidence seems to have passed on to his Chelsea team. So far.

Four English teams into the last 16 of the Champions League, followed by Germany 3, Italy 3, Spain 2, France 2, Portugal 1, Holland 1. So hasn't England done well this season. And I expect Chelsea and Man United to go further still.

But I fear for Liverpool, so limp unless Steven Gerrard is fired up, and Arsenal, nowhere as strong without Patrick Vieira on top form, which he hasn't been for most of the season, and also their habit of underachieving in Europe, a mental block they don't look like shifting. All the same, I am very excited. Plus there's Newcastle and Boro in the Uefa Cup. Gosh, a lot to look forward to in the rest of this season.

But first, I'm looking forward to my hols in the Bahamas, visiting Ocean Club, Kamalame Cay and Pink Sands. See you in February.

Every Monday, national dailies devote over 200,000 words to football

14 February 2005

FOR ABOUT THE PAST FIVE YEARS I'VE BEEN TELLING people, including myself, that for the best football coverage you should read the broadsheets not the tabloids. There's been a social upheaval, thanks to the middle classes coming into footer, which is reflected in the newspapers. Usually, for about the past hundred years, it was the downmarket papers that were most obsessed by football. Now it's the posh papers. But have I made up this wisdom, based on superficial glimpses of one or two papers? Yeah, actually. Been too lazy to do any proper research, repeating it to myself 'til I've been convinced it's true.

I happened to be having lunch with a friend who is a TV executive and he was saying he had someone on work experience coming in the following week. He never liked to give them things like tea-making and photocopying, but on the other hand it was hard to give them proper work, so they ended up, at least for the first few days, just sitting around.

"I know," I said, "I've got a project. On Monday morning"—a big day for football coverage—"give him every national newspaper and tell him to analyse their sports pages." The day in question was 6 December 2004, a fairly typical Monday, as there was no England match or big European game to skew the coverage.

I told Peter Halewood, the work-experience person in question, aged 23, graduate in media communications from the University of Gloucester, that I wanted to know which papers devoted the most space to football. As with all raw statistics, it takes time to make sense of Peter's figures (see table). For a start, what do you mean by space? Tabloid pages have fewer words, bigger pictures, bigger headlines than broadsheet pages. (And, of course, by "broadsheets" we now refer to a species, not size any more). Pages also contain adverts, and sometimes a mixture of sports. So we had to count column inches. But here are the main conclusions.

Coverage: the basic facts

Most sports pages. Sun 41, *Times* 40, *Mirror* 36.

Highest percentages devoted to sport of paper's total pages. Sun 47 per cent, *Mirror* 45 per cent, *Star* 38 per cent, *Times* 33 per cent.

Most pages devoted to football. Sun 28, *Mirror* and *Times* 24. All three have pull-out football sections.

Highest percentages of sports pages devoted to football. Sun and *Mirror* 85 per cent each, *Star* 70 per cent, *Times* and *Indie* 60 per cent.

Next-highest sports coverage after football. Horse racing was next in five papers, rugby union in four. All other sports were a long way behind football, except in the *Telegraph*.

Number of words devoted to football. I didn't get Peter to count actual words, or he would have been on work experience for the rest of his life. Instead, we estimated that an average sports page in *The Sun* contained 1,000 words, *The Mirror* 1,200 words and *The Times* 1,400. *The Telegraph*, being a true broadsheet, averages many more, roughly 3,000, but that Monday it had only five pages devoted to football. So the results were: *The Times* 33,600 words, *The Mirror* 28,800, *The Sun* 28,000, *Daily Mail* 26,000, *Daily Express* 26,000, *Indie* 26,000, *The Guardian* 20,000, *Daily Telegraph* 15,000, *The Star* 15,000.

Total words devoted to football. On that particular Monday, in our nine national dailies, it came to 218,400. That's equal to three lovely novels or two lengthy biographies.

Nature of coverage. The tabloids are dominated by the Premiership and devote little space to the other leagues, apart from a few glamour teams. *The Times* covered every league and cup game, plus the Scottish Premier League. On the other hand, *The Sun* had the most comprehensive Premiership coverage, devoting two pages to each game and giving ratings for each player, masses of stats and a groovy graph that charts their previous 20 games.

First-person columns by star players seem to have disappeared. When I was a lad, every popular paper had at least one big name with his own column, even though you knew he never wrote it, probably rarely read it. That Monday, only *The Times*, out of all nine dailies, had a current player writing: Aki Riihilahti of Crystal Palace, not exactly a star, but his column is excellent. He writes it himself, in English—and he's Finnish. The reason, presumably, is that star players, and their agents, now earn such fortunes that they can't be arsed even to answer the phone to sweaty hacks.

The *Star*, *Mirror* and *Sun* are the most opinionated in their match reports, and the most abusive, rubbishing players for being useless, fat, missing sitters—and yet they're ever so coy when it comes to rude quotations such as "I don't give a f***" or "the ref was full of bull****". *The Times* also never uses swear words, but in the *Indie* and *Guardian*, fucking hell, anything goes.

The wittiest, most amusing coverage was in the *Mirror*. Many articles, plus headlines, appeared to have been created purely for their comic value. For example, having mocked Harry Kewell in its Liverpool match report for being overweight, a side column in the paper revealed he was doing advertising for a well-known Australian biscuit called Tim Tams. It then listed other players who might do biscuit advertising: Arsenal's goalie Manuel Almunia could do Cadbury's Fingers, Everton could do Wagon Wheels—as their wheels are about to fall off—and Gary McAllister could do Garibaldi biscuits. Gerrit? *The Times* has some good funny stuff in its Hairdryer column, which is all fictional, while *The Guardian* has Clogger, which is full of jokey comments.

Best paper for football. Is a value judgement, of course,

depending on which you are used to, which writers you happen to like, what amuses you.

I asked Peter for his favourite. "I can see that *The Times* and *Guardian* are the most informative and best written, but if I had to pick just one paper for football on a Monday, it would be *The Sun*. I think its coverage is excellent. Next would be *The Mirror*." My own choice is *The Times*—but only on a Monday for The Game section, which is first-class: so much info, coverage and good ideas. On a Saturday, I prefer *The Guardian*. Other days, I read the *Indie*, but that's partly habit and loyalty.

We looked at only one day, but I was right on my general assumption. Factually, *The Times* came out best for football coverage. But aren't we lucky these days, we footer fans? So much space, attention, intelligence, research and wit gets devoted in all the dailies to our special interests.

I've just had my holiday. After hearing Motty, I need another one

21 February 2005

FOUR WEEKS AWAY, SO WHAT'S CHANGED? NOT ME. Worst West Indian hol we've had in twenty Januaries: horrible weather, bloody cold, then I got a throat infection and couldn't even drink. But the street has enjoyed it, barely able to keep a straight face and affect deep sympathy while I've been moaning on.

James Beattie, it was strange seeing him come on for Everton against Chelsea. Funny things, eyes: they get accustomed to registering certain players for certain clubs in certain strips. No sooner got my brain reprogrammed than he was off, for head-butting someone—in the back of the head. That was unusual. I've never quite understood the physiological theory of head-butting, the head-to-head sort. Surely, you must hurt yourself as much as the other girl. Or does the fact that you know you are going to do it somehow insulate or anaesthetise you? José Mourinho loved it, of course, sitting there smug and snug in his coat, the same one he's been wearing for twenty Januaries. Has he not heard of Oxfam?

There was another strange incident when he sent on a sub carrying a handwritten note for Cardoso Tiago, presumably in Portuguese. Never seen that before, but it's sensible. No player can hear a manager screaming and shouting. Coaches should hold up notices and save their voices. The instructions for penalties and free-kicks would be in code, so that the other team wouldn't understand. Eventually, of course, each player will have a chip under his skin, undetectable by the ref. Then they can be controlled like robots.

The pitch at Goodison Park was terrible. I felt I'd been projected back twenty years. It's been a mild winter, yet so many footie pitches are cutting up. How do you know, Hunt? Swanning off to the Windies, lucky for some.

I know it because I came back and cut the lawn. It was 12 February, an all-time record, and we've lived in this house for 42 years. Whenever I did the first cutting of the year, I used to ring my father-in-law, Arthur, in Carlisle and say guess what and he'd go, "Ooohhhh." I do miss this fascinating annual conversation. He died eight years ago. But not forgotten. I told him in my head.

The referee Graham Poll has got fatter, in just four weeks, and Richard Keys of Sky TV, the hairy one who looks as if he has to shave on the hour, has put on four years. I heard a new phrase, emerging from the lips of two different people—Niall Quinn and Chris Coleman, each chuntering on about the unlikelihood of some team coming back, or someone scoring: "It's a big ask." Behind my back, they've turned a verb into a noun. I look forward to hearing it in a West Indian accent, when it will come out as a "big arcs".

I got back in time to watch England against Holland.

What a mistake. So depressing, and I needed cheering up after my luxury hol. I never thought Sven had it, but whatever he had has gone. The world and his hamster can now see the king clearly has no clothes. Sven has pulled off the biggest con trick in football. He has no ideas, no skills, no energy. The FA gave him the job on the rebound for two simple reasons—he wasn't over excitable like Kevin Keegan or mad like Glenn Hoddle. Let's have a sponge, they decided. Now he's so soggy he should be wrung out.

To add to my groans, the commentator was John Motson, may God spare us, still suffering from false-laughter syndrome. He has this trick of clearing his throat, then giving a little chuckle when nothing remotely amusing has happened or been said, least of all by him. Then he starts trotting out inane facts he has laboriously written down beforehand in his best joined-up handwriting. He revealed that Stewart Downing, making his debut, was the first Middlesbrough-born player, while actually playing for Middlesbrough, where he was born, and in their team—oh, do get on with it, John—to appear for England in forty years! Astounding.

Watching England, thinking about Sven, then having to listen to Motty, it was doing ma' fucking head in, as Gazza used to tell me all the time. What I need is a holiday.

It's your lucky day, I told him. I've got a spare ticket, only 50 quid

28 February 2005

FOR THREE DAYS I'D BEEN RINGING PEOPLE SAYING I'd got a spare ticket for Arsenal, top seat, West Stand Upper, only £50, who wants it. I'd already paid my friend for it, the one from whom I rent a half-season ticket, as he was going to be away. I thought I'd take my son, as a treat, though he hates Arsenal, being a true Spurs fan, unlike some he could name (i.e., his old man). But he couldn't make it. I tried two people in our street, who always boast that they are Arsenal fans, with no luck. I left a message for Ken Loach, who lives behind us. He likes football and is not prejudiced, but by 11.30 he hadn't replied, so off I went with my next-door neighbours in a minicab, clutching my spare ticket.

The traffic was terrible. The driver, who smelled strongly of aftershave and had a large "I Love Jesus" sticker on his dashboard, got stuck taking a daft detour, but all I could think about was my spare ticket. The waiting list for Arsenal season tickets is 20 years.

I can't possibly throw away fifty quid. Oh what a mess. I won't even be able to tell my wife. I'm the one in this house who goes on constantly about waste. I could sell it to a tout, and they will get £100 for it, but then some poor sod will have to sit next to me and I'll feel guilty he's been ripped off.

We were running so late that I realised we'd miss kick-off, so I was leaning over the driver's shoulder, begging him to hurry up, when I noticed in the corner of his window a little sticker—for Arsenal. Beside him, rolled up, was a baseball cap with the Gunners symbol.

He was an Arsenal fan, had followed them for 14 years since coming from Ghana—but had never gone to a game. I said it's your lucky day. I have a spare ticket, only £50. He made a face. His wife would never forgive him. He would lose two hours' work. With four young children and a rental to the cab firm of £120 a week in cash to find, he couldn't afford not to work all day. Anyway, what would he do with his own car?

Good point. The reason we'd taken a minicab was that you can't park, not for a Saturday game. Prue from next door, who was going to her first football match, said what about Waitrose car park? It's free for two hours, and then it's only £10, which she said she'd pay. The driver sighed, his eyes turned upwards longingly, but no, he just couldn't. I said OK, then. You can have my ticket for nothing. Still he said no.

We were in sight of the new stadium when we hit another huge traffic jam. The driver turned down a side street—and we found ourselves at the entrance to the Waitrose car park. It's a sign, I said. Jesus has spoken. He held his arms up in the air, clutched his forehead, then parked the car.

As we walked to the ground, he started ringing his

friends, his wife and children, telling them he was on his way to Highbury, speaking half in English, half in Twi. He's an Akan, he said, the majority people of Ghana. Several times he handed the phone to me so I could confirm that I'd given him a ticket.

He started following Arsenal when he first came to London, working as a presser in a sweatshop, because he liked Paul Davis and Michael Thomas. Although he'd never seen a game, he did visit Highbury every year—to buy an Arsenal calendar to hang up in his house in Leyton. His own children follow Aston Villa and Man U. Eventually, he wants to retire to Ghana. The thought of living there appals his children, though they like it for hols.

Arsenal, being a foreign team, does have one Ghanaian, Quincy Owusu-Abeyie, but he wasn't playing. Marcel Desailly, ex-France and Chelsea, born in Ghana, is a national hero, said my new friend. Throughout the match, he was either jumping up and down, laughing and clapping, or on his mobile, letting his friends hear the crowd roaring. At half-time, I took his photo with his phone, proof that he'd been there.

It was quite a boring game, 1–1 in the Cup against Sheffield United, but not to him. And I was pleased by his pleasure.

Not like me to be so generous, so my dear wife kindly pointed out when I came home. You've got me wrong, I said, glowing with virtue. It's good to be good. We're all one nation in football.

My wife lingers over photos of Mourinho, especially that moody one

7 March 2005

CAN'T WAIT FOR THE WEEK AHEAD, FOR THE SECOND legs of the UEFA Champions League. I do love this time of the season, when there are so many ace Euro games and so many ace English clubs still in. OK, half in. Who would have thought that Liverpool would be the only one of our four to be ahead after the first leg? Well, most of Europe, probably. One thing all these games show us is that the Spanish and the Italian leagues are better.

It's been exhausting, of course, and will be in the week ahead, flicking between the channels. It's so annoying having two big games, two nights running, going on at the same time. Poor old Gordon Brown. I hope his video worked, the one he set when he had to drag himself off to China.

In the first leg, I chose to watch Chelsea *v* Barcelona rather than Manchester United *v* A C Milan, but they flash the other score up, so you know what's going on anyway. When there was a hold-up, or even just a throw-in or goal kick, I found myself switching over to the other game for an update. At half-times, you hope to catch up on what you've missed, which is hard, because the buggers synchronise the commercials. It also means you never have time to go to the lav. I can see commodes coming back, if this goes on. In your favourite club colours, of course.

I did a little survey next day whenever I met a human being, from the postie to people who rang, asking them who they watched first, Chelsea or Man United. Mainly it seemed to be Man United. For the uncommitted, they are on better form, playing more positively.

People on the phone also had a question for me: What's it like being the only Hunter left in the western world? You what, I said first time they asked, not knowing that Hunter S Thompson had died. It was strange, seeing the headline "Hunter shoots himself". Exactly my age as well. Mothers must have taken a sudden fancy to Hunter that year. Two anyway. The only other one I have heard of in my lifetime was a footballer called Hunter Devine. I think he played for Queens Park, the Glasgow club. And I think he was called Devine. More spottings, please.

Naturally, I chose Chelsea for José Mourinho. I am fascinated by him, though not as much as my dear wife. She thinks he's gorgeous. Oh no, gerroff, stopit, that's my sore arm. I'm just winding you up. But she always seems to linger over photographs of him, specially that moody one of him, seen through snowflakes, unshaven, his collar up like a Fifties French film star, oooh, Ivy. People are comparing him to Brian Clough, but Cloughy had the sexual attraction of a plate.

We all knew that the arrival of Roman Abramovich would dramatically shake up the Premiership, not allowing Man United and Arsenal to have it their own way, which has been good, but we didn't expect him to hire a Chelsea manager who would turn out to be a drama in himself. He can't resist shooting his mouth off, telling us how clever and smart and successful he is. He endlessly amuses me, but the football hacks are about to turn against him, having worked so hard to build him up.

I'll be going to the Arsenal-Bayern Munich game. I expect the Gunners to be crap, just as they always are in Europe, further proof that our Premiership is not as good as Sky TV tells us. But I'll still enjoy it. The crowds are brilliant at European matches, singing all the way through. That's the Germans. Arsenal fans will go very quiet.

One of the puzzles about Europe is Dennis Bergkamp. We know he doesn't fly and so he misses the away legs, but what does he do? Practise keepy-uppy in his garden? Take the wife for a walk round the block? What about his contract? Presumably it's written in that he's let off flying, but does he therefore lose out on the bonuses? Next time I sign a book contract to write someone's biography I'll say sorry, I don't travel, you'll have to come to me. But not during the footer. I'll be busy.

On Wednesday, at Highbury, I'll be watching carefully in case some kid drops that huge circular tablecloth they shake before kick-off, and also listening to the Euro anthem. Just to check if they really are singing, "Lasagne!"

Surely there must be a therapist who could talk me out of this obsession

14 March 2005

NINE MONTHS AGO, I AGREED TO GIVE A TALK AT 'Words by the Water', a literary festival in Keswick. I said I would never do another, waste of time, what's the point, I've got better things to do, such as nothing, but two Cumbrian friends twisted my arm. I knew the moment I said I would that I'd regret it. I didn't know why. I just knew that when the weekend in question approached, I would be effing and blinding.

It was last Friday, 4 March, I gave my little talk. Two, in fact. As I'm never doing any again, ever ever, I decided to give them their money's worth. Correction: there was no money, just a free meal, bed and breakfast. As if I can't get free meals here, at home. That's what my dear wife does. And she never charges.

I chose a Friday, as that's usually the poorest day for football on TV. Turned out that Burnley were playing Sunderland. OK, not Premiership, and neither is a team I support, though I have a soft spot for Sunderland and would like to see them back in the Premiership. It was apparently a good game, damn and blast, and Sunderland went to the top of the Championship, buggerit.

But I carefully planned it so that I'd travel back by train first thing Saturday morning, well in time for Arsenal at home to Portsmouth. Yes, I'm a Spurs fan, but surely the game didn't matter. And Portsmouth are pretty boring. But I was desperate to go. I've got my half-season ticket to Highbury, innit?

Bloody Virgin Trains. They have decided to work on the West Coast Main Line at weekends, so I couldn't get a train from Penrith. I persuaded one of the festival helpers to drive me all the way to Darlington, right across the Pennines, in deepest snow, in order to pick up the East Coast line. Which I did, but not in time to get myself to Highbury.

Our three children now live within walking distance of our London house, which is great. I get to see my two grandchildren all the time. Yet when they arrive for Sunday lunch, which is a fixed family event, I find myself jumping up from the table, pretending to fetch something, and then rushing to my room where I have left Sky on at full blast, just to check the score.

If there's only one match on a Sunday, kick-off at four, that's fine—I can enjoy a leisurely lunch with my dear children and grandchildren, whom of course I adore, light of my life, tra la. But when it's a lunchtime kick-off, oh God, do I moan.

Now and again, about once a millennium, my wife wants to invite Derek and Sue, or Prue and Ian, our neighbours on either side, to supper. I say OK, pet, fine by me. But not a Saturday or Sunday, please. Oh, and certainly not a Monday, as there's always a good Premiership game.

Tuesday, Wednesday and Thursday, they're out. Could well be a European game. A Friday's not bad. Hold on. Depends which one: they show a Championship game on a Friday. Could be vital for play-offs. I know—could we put it off till the end of the season? In fact, this summer's fine. But don't fix anything for next summer, 'cos it's the World Cup.

The point of telling you all this trivia is because it is so totally utterly pathetic. How can a grown man, with so much richness in his life, allow himself to be dominated by something so stupid as football? Ruby and Amelia, my grandchildren, are only five. A delightful age. They'll be grown up soon, refusing to come to Sunday lunch. I'll have missed their childhood years by sitting in front of the telly shouting "Goal!" or "Rubbish!"

Do I need help? Places like the Priory, where Gazza went, will help you with addictions like drink or drugs. By chance, I met the boss of the Priory recently on holiday in the Bahamas. Wonder if he'd do me a discount. There are also experts to help if you are besotted by sex, smoking, gambling.

Surely, there must be a football therapist by now, one who will talk you out of your obsession. Probably consists of watching 1970s videos of John Pratt shooting over the West Stand into Tottenham High Road—until you scream for mercy, promising never to watch a game again.

Yours, worried, Brown Eye.

I buy cheapo Penny Black stamps; Wenger buys very thin, cheapo kids

21 March 2005

ABOUT 20 YEARS AGO, I BECAME A BORN-AGAIN stamp collector. By born-again, I mean I collected them as a boy, then forgot about them for decades. I was so busy with other things. Such as living. This is typical of many stamp collectors. What sparked me off again was giving up playing weekend football. I just could not bear to see the lads playing without me. I thought, what shall I do now? Is there a hobby which isn't going to knacker my poor old knees any more?

For about ten years, I collected GB stamps, including a special collection of Wembley 1924–25 stamps. I also collected US Columbus stamps and GB covers for the postmarks, mainly 19th-century Cumbrian. Oh, lots of daft things. Too many, really. That's what born-agains do. Rush at things.

Today, I collect stamps on one theme only—football. The earliest football stamp, as you've asked (i.e., a stamp connected with football), was issued by Uruguay in 1924 to celebrate their footie victory in the 1924 Olympics. It doesn't actually show a footballer. The earliest of these came out from Bulgaria in 1931.

One of the things I used to collect was penny blacks. These are not as expensive as you might think, as 68 million were printed. I specialised in cheapo blacks with thins (meaning the paper had got thin over the years) and poor margins (meaning no margins, and a good black should have four white margins). I paid no more than £20 each, as opposed to £200 for a decent black in good nick. I collected them for their letters (oh, I'm too tired to explain what that means). To me, the condition didn't really matter much. It was having them that mattered.

When I came to sell, I lost money on every one. Now, if I had been a sensible collector, splashed out and gone for tried and proven quality, I would have bought one half-decent black at £200 instead of ten tatty ones at £20. I would then have doubled my money over ten years. Are you getting my drift. Are you with me. Or ahead. Yes, friends, isn't that just like football?

During January, while my back was turned, Martin Jol of Spurs bought nine cheapo players, most of whom I had never heard of. All a bit thin, and poor at the margins, I'm sure. This was in addition to the 15 new signings earlier in the season. Spurs now have 36 players in the first-team squad, enough for three teams, yet I haven't personally seen half of them on the pitch yet. I'm dying to see a defender called Defendi; read the back of Emil Hallfredsson's shirt, as I'm sure they'll miss out some letters; and salaam to Mounir el-Hamdaoui. As it is, I wouldn't recognise any of them if they turned up in my porridge.

Arsène Wenger has also gone for bargain basements, buying unknown kids, all of them very thin. Several of these have in fact appeared and done quite well—Francesc Fabregas, Mathieu Flamini, Robin van Persie, Quincy Owusu-Abeyie, Jeremie Aladiere—but as the season went on, most of them faded. José Antonio Reyes cost a bit of money, but he hasn't proved to be a bargain, so far.

Wenger, in reality, keeps on buying the same, as I did with my cheapo blacks. He has a clutch of midfield players, young, inexperienced, white, slender, medium height, dark-haired, vaguely Latin, who look much the same. When I stare across to the bench to see who's coming on, I can't tell the difference. Or even when they get on the pitch. At the moment, Wenger has £30m to spend, so we are told, but then he's had this mythical money for two years. Will he be able to change the habits of a lifetime, go against his personality, and splash out on one real, proven, top-quality player at the height of his powers? Or will he buy ten cheapo players, hoping that one will come good?

Alex Ferguson has always been willing to splash out on top players, like Rio Ferdinand and Wayne Rooney. Ah, you say, hasn't done him much good, not this season. Well, Man United would have done even worse without them. But the main point is that, like a good penny black, if you buy proven quality, like Ferdinand and Rooney, you'll more easily get your money back.

When a player gets sent off, shouldn't we fans get some money back?

28 March 2005

THERE ARE SO MANY THINGS I HATE, BEING A FOOTball fan. Getting to the ground, that's a real drag, whether by public transport or by car. Got so much worse these past few years. Football programmes, what a waste of money. And the nasty, overpriced tea and coffee in nasty plastic cups, ugh, do I not like them.

Players wearing gloves, what jessies, how can they? Players wearing black armbands because some director you've never heard of has died, or there's been a terrible disaster. Not outside in Tottenham High Road, or Highbury Fields, or in the middle of Stanley Park, or on the edge of Trafford Park, but all because something awful happened ten thousand miles away across the globe and it's just been on the news. If I want to grieve for the victims, as well I might, I don't need some craven football club to tell me how and when.

TV football commentators who promise us that at half-time there will be some "talking points", which you know fine well will be proof that the ref or linesman gave a throw-in to the wrong side, no, really—or video replays which will show that a goal kick was not actually over the line, wow, did you ever. A "big talking point" means a penalty disallowed. A "major talking point" will be handbags and hisses at three feet. I sit there, stunned by the pointlessness of it all, and shout, "No one is talking about any of these in our house, so belt up!"

But what really, really does seriously upset me is Ten Men. Once I see a red card being brandished, and a player about to leave the field, very slowly, effing and blinding, turning and cursing, stopping and slobbering, I immediately want to give up. Whether I'm at the game, or watching on telly, I think: That's it, might as well pack up, the game's ruined.

Now it is true, on some occasions, that the team reduced to ten men plays better. Spurred on by the injustice of it all, or a backs-to-the-wall mentality, the remaining ten often give 10 per cent more. And often that equals 100 per cent, or a new player. Ergo, it's now back to eleven *v* eleven.

But it rarely works that way. The team reduced usually substitutes another man, often taking off its best attacker, rearranges its formation, chucks away its game plan, and tries to hang on to what it's got, if anything at all, or attempts to minimise the chances of being stuffed.

The team on the park with 11 men relaxes, thinking it's going to be a doddle, while the team manager, knowing how stupid footballers are, tries to counter this by tinkering with his own formation to parry the changes the opposition has made.

Either road up, the game is immediately a nonsense, excitement goes, expectations on either side drain away. The game we'd all turned up to see has gone.

In the past couple of weeks, when Didier Drogba got sent off in Chelsea's first-leg Champions League game against Barcelona, the effect on Chelsea was to become tired rather than inspired. When Olympiakos, in the first leg of the Uefa Cup against Newcastle, went down to nine men, Newcastle still didn't play any better.

I often wonder if we can sue for compensation, we football fans. We have paid for our season ticket, or our Sky subscription, to watch a game clearly billed in the programme as eleven against eleven. We have thus been short-changed when one team ends up a man down. Could we claim one-twenty-second of our money back? Not piddling, when you think Premiership fans are paying £1,000 a year.

Alternatively, teams could behave like the Corinthians used to do, back in the 1900s. They were the totally amateur, public-school, Oxbridge team that put fair play and moral values above such sordid, vulgar things as winning. They never argued with the ref or entered any competition where there was a prize. If by chance the other team lost a man, either sent off or through injury, they immediately and voluntarily sent off one of their own men, just to keep things even.

Jose, are you listening? You're supposed to be cool. Why not try it next time it happens to Chelsea? You'd win house points.

In 1920, Goodison Park had 53,000 fans for a women's football match

4 April 2005

MOST MEN HAVEN'T QUITE GOT USED TO WOMEN IN football. They are still surprised by females sounding knowledgeable about footer on the radio and TV or writing in the papers.

They look along the rows of seats in the stands and think, hmm, that's funny, I can see women — who let them in? Or, in the pub, they are shocked upon hearing them argue the toss about last night's game, or why that wanker Beckham is now a peripheral figure and should be dropped by Sven.

Nor have they got used to seeing them actually playing the game, in schools and clubs all over the country. Or live on TV, which we'll see a lot of this summer, as England will be hosting the finals of the European Women's Championship. Fifa reckons that by 2010 there will be more women in the world playing football than men. And yet women in football is not a new thing. I often amuse myself, when looking through my football memorabilia, by examining old crowd shots. If you peer hard enough, you will always find some female fans.

In a report of the Queen's Park *v* Wanderers game at

Hampden Park in 1875, it was noted, "4,000 spectators turned up, including many ladies". For the FA Cup final of 1905, a group of female fans calling themselves the Newcastle Ladies Final Outing Club arranged a trip to London to cheer on United, hiring their own carriage on the train.

In 1895, the British Ladies Football Club was formed in London, holding its first game at Crouch End athletics ground. The secretary and captain was Miss Nettie J Honeyball. What a name—surely she should have been in a James Bond film—and what a gel. I have her photo pinned up before me in her full football gear—baggy knickerbockers, real football boots as used by men, and a massive pair of shin guards, worn outside the socks, as all players did in those days. The pioneers of women's football were poshos, the club's first president being Lady Florence Dixie, daughter of the Marquess of Queensberry. Then, as in the men's game, the working classes took over.

In 1914, when the First World War broke out, more than one million women went to work in the munitions factories. They were soon replacing the men on the football pitch as well, organising their own teams to play against other factories. In 1920, it was estimated there were 150 women's teams. All the proceeds from their games went to charity.

The most famous, most successful women's team—of all time, really, as no modern version has had better support—was Dick Kerr's Ladies. I used to think their manager must have been a bloke called Dick Kerr, but their name came from W B Dick and John Kerr, founders of a large factory in Preston which made tramways, moving into munitions when the war started. They played local games at first, then travelled further afield. In 1919, about 35,000 turned up to watch them against Newcastle Ladies at St James's Park. They did a French tour, attracting crowds of 20,000 on average at each game.

Dick Kerr's biggest gate came on 23 December 1920, when they played St Helen's Ladies at Goodison, Everton's ground, watched by 53,000. Every time I tell this fact to any football fan, male or female, they can't believe it.

In 1921, however, those bastards at the FA banned the women's game. They maintained football was a man's game, unsuitable for the female body. Funny, that. Young women had been considered fit and strong enough to man munitions factories, but now they couldn't kick a ball about. The FA also alleged some fiddling of expenses with their contributions to charities. It wasn't true, and even if it were, men had been fiddling around with the money pouring into football from the very beginning. And still are.

So that was it, really, for the next 50 years. Women's football was finally recognised by the FA in 1971, and in 1993 the FA took over responsibility for the women's game in England.

In this summer's competition, England are expected to do quite well. They could reach the semi-finals. And I'll be watching. Let's hope the lasses done good.

Join the friends of Becks for a discount on Brylcreem

11 April 2005

I'M GOING INTO THE ROYAL FREE HOSPITAL, GEORGE and Mary ward, no grapes, please, to have a new knee. Never liked this one. Should have traded it in years ago. All my own fault. Despite having had two cartilage ops, I played football 'til I was 50, which was stupid. One op was never really successful. Hence this dodgy knee I've been carrying around with me.

Bad timing. It's Euro week, with Chelsea and Liverpool both playing. But if I come round in time, still in one piece, having managed not to catch a superbug, maybe I can watch the Chelsea game. I wonder if George and Mary has Sky?

Worst of all, I'm going to miss the first annual meeting of the FoB. I was thrilled when it was formed, just before England's last World Cup qualifying games. So many people were being really horrible about David, saying he should be dropped. How could they be so stupid? But David showed them, didn't he just. What a magnificent goal he scored against the giants of Azerbaijan. Some small-minded people said he was offside, and he had only the goalie to beat, but that is sooo silly.

The Friends of Becks, well, it's like Friends of the Tate. Members get a discount on various items, like Brylcreem, and a limited-edition print of Brooklyn's tree house, which cost only £250,000. The tree house, I mean. Not the print. That's authenticated by Tony Stephens, David's agent. Shows it's kosher. There's an FoB newsletter, which is really good. And, of course, access to a website. That's where I first heard about it.

It started because of all the petty, unfair criticisms he's been having recently. Those who truly love and adore him wanted to rally round, show support.

First, people have been saying he's the reason Real Madrid have been rubbish this season. If you ask me, that fat Brazilian up front, he's the real problem, plus that baldy Frenchman. They've done nothing while David has worked his socks off. Then for England, some have even said he shouldn't be captain, as he can't run, can't head the ball, can't tackle, can't beat his man, chickens out of tackles, then throws himself at the nearest player when he loses the ball. All of which is so untrue. David never loses the ball. Lesser people take it off him.

He's also had all that unpleasant stuff about his personal life: that girl whose name I'm not going to mention. He's already said it's ludicrous. Isn't that enough?

Then his hair. He can't win. If he changes its colour and style all the time, he gets mocked. Now that he's just letting it grow, alfresco, al dente, people are saying, ahh, we can see he has boring, mousy hair—and it's receding. Aren't people horrid?

As members of the FoB, one of the things we all had to do after that Northern Ireland game (yes, he did play, don't be sarky, his name was definitely on the team sheet) was to send personal e-mails to all the papers. We got given the name of the idiot on each paper who does the ratings — you know, marks out of ten for performance. I just could not believe so many people gave David just five points. One gave him only three. Blind, or what? We were told not to send any death threats. Just sort of heavy warnings: we know where you live, the names of your kids.

Sven is president of the FoB. It's well known that he's madly in love with David, always will be. You can see it in his eyes. Motty is vice-president, bless.

Julie Burchill is one of our patrons. She did that lovely little book about him a few years ago. People were horrid at the time, so jealous, saying she was just cashing in, she'd missed the boat, it was a cuttings job, she wouldn't recognise a football if one landed in her knickers. Or two. She's a big girl.

She'll be at the meeting. Such a shame I'll miss it. I was hoping to get her views on the offside trap, whether David was or not. Alex Ferguson was asked to give the inaugural lecture. What an honour. Can't understand how he's got a prior engagement.

Anyway, David, I'll be thinking of you as I go under. Before Mr Dowd, he's my surgeon, starts operating. Kissy, kissy. George and Mary, it's on the eighth floor. Just in case you're passing.

He may have mumbled, but Gazza thanked me. Rare glory for a ghost!

2 May 2005

I GOT A HUGE BUNCH OF FLOWERS WHILE IN hospital which came from David Beckham. His signature on the card was very clear. How thoughtful of him. I made sure the whole ward read it. It did improve my stock. Up until then, most of the patients had marked me down as a right moaner.

First of all, hospitals have this new thing called patient line, new since the last time I was in the Royal Free, which was 1979. It's an individual phone, TV and radio system, very dinky, which hangs over each bed. Very handy, if bloody expensive. I seemed to be pouring £2 TV cards into it all the time—and still failed to get any football. They have some cable channels, most of which I've never heard of, but no Sky Sports.

The radio part is free, oh so generous, but it turned out not to provide Radio 5 Live. Isn't that daft? Such a popular, professional channel, combining news and sport, all very slick, perfect for lying in bed, moaning, yet they don't have it.

In my ward, the George and Mary, I seemed mostly to be surrounded by these really old blokes who had had knee or hip replacements. On close examination, they turned out to be, well, around my own age, i.e., not at all old. They were slumped most of the day, with no interest in vital things like football scores. Or they just lay there, snoring. After a hip or knee op, you have to lie on your back, not your side, which is how most people sleep. Hence all the horrendous snoring. Not from me, of course. Neither an oldie nor a snorer let me be.

Then I realised I was never going to make that big do at the Grosvenor House Hotel for the British Book Awards, where the very excellent book about Gazza was on the shortlist for the sports book of the year. I'd got my ticket and was looking forward to getting drunk at the publisher's expense, though not, of course, in front of Gazza. He's not had a drink for two years.

In my fantasy world, I'd intended to be up and about, no bother, once the op was over. I never expected the pain and the swelling to be so hellish and to last for so long. But then I did have a total knee replacement. It's a huge thing, made of plastic stuff and silvery-looking steel, which I saw before they put it in. My weight must now be up by about half a stone, carrying it around.

However, I did manage to see the hour-long TV prog, introduced by Richard and Judy, and devoted to the book awards, on Channel 4. And Gazza did win. In his acceptance speech, which most people on the ward could hardly understand, as he did mumble, he clearly mentioned my name. Oh yes he did. You deaf, or what? He thanked me for helping him write the book. Which was nice.

How life has moved on for ghost-writers. At one time,

they didn't get their name mentioned anywhere. Sometimes they never even got to meet the person they were writing about.

In 1978, during the World Cup finals in Argentina, at the time of Ally's Tartan Army, when Scotland got there but England didn't, there was a hack on the Sun who wrote a ghosted daily column as if written by one of the Scottish stars. Yet during the whole of the World Cup, he never met or spoke to him once. The hack made it all up while the star took the money, not caring what appeared under his name.

There were one or two blokes on my ward who'd been slightly cynical about my flowers from the Blessed David, but when I explained about the Gazza book, and that I really did know him, that's how you do these books, they were quite impressed. I came out of the hospital with my head held quite high, even if I was trailing my bloody left leg behind me, still moaning.

Late flash: Just faxed this column across, as I don't have e-mail, can't trust the post, and pigeons are just so slow. P Wilby, the ed, then rang to welcome me back, asked about my knee and if I got the flowers OK.Oh, God, it was he who sent them. Not Becks. Bastard. Not a word to George and Mary.

Mourinho shows that even rubbish players can get respect as managers

9 May 2005

THAT'S IT THEN, ALMOST. ANOTHER SEASON DRAWing to a close. Another load of memories and images, highlights 'n' lowlights, talking points and tunnel incidents to be carefully stashed away and, well, lost. Now, was it last season or the season before that Arsenal went all season without, er, something or other? No, I tell a lie. It was in 1889. And Preston North End, the Invincibles. I can see them now. Ted Drake was the manager, Fatty Foulke was in goal and Brian Glanville was in short trousers, still to say his first word, which was, of course, catennacio. So, better round up this season, before it all goes yellow in the mind.

Most successful team of the season. Chelsea, obviously.

Most attractive team of the season. On form, in spells, Arsenal were more entertaining, exciting, creative. Too often Chelsea were holding on to 1–0. In that deciding game against Bolton, they were 1–0 up with 25 minutes to go when they took off their main striker, Didier Drogba, and put on that lump, Robert Huth. They were desperate to keep their fragile lead. I don't call that attractive. It's pragmatism. The London-based football hacks now love

Chelsea, going on about the magic of Damien Duff and Arjen Robben, yet they contributed so little to the season. Duff is Darren Huckerby with O-levels. Down goes his head, knows not where he's going to.

Manager of season. José Mourinho. Obviously. No competition there. He's done it with will-power, cunning, personality, not just the money. He's provided brilliant copy and also finally laid to rest that old football dressing-room cliché—"Show us your medals." Players will give managers respect even if they had rubbish or non-existent playing careers.

Team what has done bloody well. Wigan Athletic. I love it that they didn't get into the Football League 'til 1978—and yet have progressed through all the divisions. Yes, they have a sugar daddy, but a modest one compared with Roman Abramovich. There's no chance ever again of any team, like Carlisle United did in 1974, rising from the bottom division to the very top without a mega-moneybags in sight.

Tune of the season. I do like Charlton trotting out to the strains of "The red, red robin goes bob, bob, bobbin'". Makes me smile. Everton's "Z Cars", that brings a warm glow as well, and Spurs's "MacNamara's Band". Oh, what a sentimental old fool. On the other hand, if I hear those inane Man United fans singing "Oooh, ahh, Cantona" once again, I'll puke.

Nice image of the season. Several groups of Norwich City fans, old and young, men and women, taking photos of themselves standing outside Arsenal's Highbury stadium.

"You'll never play here again," some uncouth Arsenal yobs immediately started singing. I don't think it was just that. I like to imagine they were capturing a bit of football history, knowing Highbury, the stadium, will soon be no more.

Sad image of the season. Callum Davidson, veteran defender, now with Preston, who has had terrible injuries. He came off in the game against Wigan with a damaged calf. Later, we caught the briefest glimpse of him on the bench, ice pack on his leg, but it was long enough to see he was bent over, his head in both hands. "Is that it?" I could feel him thinking. Poor lad.

Commentator of the season. Big Ron has not returned, not to my living room, but Chris Kamara is creating a distinctive style for himself. In moments of excitement, he speaks not in tongues, like Big Ron, but dialogue. For example, instead of telling us, in the third person, that a player is arguing with a ref over a free-kick, he will suddenly go into the first person, imagining what each is saying. "Oi, ref, this is far enough back, innit?" "No, it's not! I'm in charge, I know what I'm doing..."

Missing person. James Beattie? Did he go to Everton? Or space?

Phrase of the season. "Little bit of afters". A mild understatement meaning that a player has tried to kill another player.

Haircut of the season. Not awarded. Beckham has had other things on his mind. Right, see you next season.

2005 – 06
SEASON

Cricket, lovely cricket,
Carlisle bounce back,
farewell Roy Keane,
hello to the Rooney
autobiography

By the end of this season, Arsène will look like Auden's love child

29 August 2005

I WAITED ALL SUMMER FOR THE NEW LEAGUE season, but thanks to Albanian under-13s, Peace Cups in Korea, War Cups in Holland, three-a-side Masters in various old folks' homes, there were only about 17 minutes this summer in which there wasn't some sort of live, or at least warmed-up, football to watch. Now we're well into the real thing. And it's so exciting, with many new things to ponder and wonder at.

Hleb of Arsenal, that thin lad with the baggy socks, the ones Steve Claridge used to wear. How do you pronounce his name? No commentator has told me yet. Do you clear your throat and have a dry spit, or is the "h" silent, as in long grass?

The sight of two of Fulham's subs on exercise bikes while they wait to come on. That's something I have never seen before. But what a good idea. Instead of sitting sulking, scratching their balls, wishing for their rival to break his leg, wanting to throttle the manager, they are doing something positive and active. There must have been long discussions about what activity would be best. Flower arranging, that's excellent therapy. Or they could sell programmes and be really useful. Knitting was considered but rejected. In case they got injured.

The Chelsea bench has, of course, been the most magnificent sight of the season so far—£78m worth of raw meat, just sitting, doing bugger all. Didier Drogba, Michael Essien and Shaun Wright-Phillips have been bought for fortunes, mainly for decorative purposes. Poor old Joe Cole, worth only half a fortune, has had to sit up in the stand, unseen. It's like those mad billionaires who buy Old Masters, then lock them in vaults.

At least an Old Master's value will increase—but Young Football Millionaires become a decreasing asset, growing old and mouldy, bitter and twisted, their confidence going, their image tainted.

Arsène is getting more lined. By the end of the season, he'll look like W H Auden's love child. Mourinho has let his hair grow, but is now shaving on match days. Fergie gets redder and Fergier.

Gold is the new white, as Private Eye would say. Suddenly numbers on shirts have gone golden, as at Arsenal, Newcastle and elsewhere. Someone has worked a nice concession.

Frank Lampard still has to work on his tum. He kicked off the season looking plumpen and lumpen, clearly having enjoyed himself too much in the summer. That's what happens when you get Best in Show awards. The rot sets in, or self-satisfaction.

Spurs top of the League. Blimey. Blink and you'll miss it.

Michael Owen has gone awfully thin-faced. What can the matter be? No one loves him? All the benches are occupied?

It's strange how players develop at different rates. Certain youngsters suddenly shoot forward, seem mature and polished beyond their years, appear destined for greatness, then sort of slow down, get stuck, get found out. Wayne Rooney is clearly keeping it up, but players like Kieron Dyer, Gareth Barry, Glen Johnson, excellent when they first emerged, have not really progressed in the past two years. This season, I have fears for Jermaine Jenas and Shaun Wright-Phillips. I suspect their best might still be a long time ahead of them.

I've already had enough of Brian Marwood's expert commentary. His expertise is in saying a lot of words, all of them empty or clichéd. "It would have been in, if it had gone in." Is that what I heard him say last week? I definitely heard the follow-up: "And the whole complex of the game would have changed."

As for manager-speak, only a few days now 'til the end of the transfer deadline, when we'll no longer hear "we're just three players short of a good squad". In the case of Portsmouth, Wigan and Sunderland, at this moment in time, Brian, each of them is just 11 players short of a good team.

Oh yes, I'll be blaming Sven if England fail at the World Cup

5 September 2005

IS IT BECAUSE WE IS RUBBISH AT FOOTBALL? IS THAT why more people are watching cricket? I have found myself turning over to the Test, despite not really knowing the rules or recognising the faces. There is something mesmerising. I'll just watch another over, I tell myself, then another. Something is bound to happen soon, or in the next five days, and I'll kick myself if I miss it, whatever it was. The graphics make me smile, as does the bloke who sits by his computer to explain LBW. All this amazing technology for something so piddling as a ball hitting a bat. Or not.

Cricket has gone working class, since last I took much interest. The players are wearing proper white pullies, so that's something, and white long 'uns, but none of them seems to have gone to a decent public school or captained Oxford, judging by the accents. And my dear, the crowds are full of lager-swilling yobs. Where are all the middle classes? In the posh seats at Chelsea or Arsenal, that's where.

Big, world-class events—Wimbledon, or Open golf, or a Test against the Aussies—are bound to get a lot of attention if they are exciting and some of our lads might do well.

Afterwards, most of us forget about it for another year. It always surprises me when I see a photo of Tim Henman somewhere else in the world. Goodness, I think, don't say he plays tennis all the year round.

With all this exciting cricket, coinciding with the new footer season, there is a backlash against our spoiled, too-rich, too-pampered Premiership stars and obscenely wealthy clubs, such as Chelsea, bulldozing their way to the top. But the real reason for any discontent with football is that we are rubbish. The England team, I mean. The humiliating defeat by Denmark will not be forgotten quickly, even if we manage in the next few days to stuff the giants of Wales and Northern Ireland.

In point of fact, England has been rubbish for 40 years, not even making the final of a world or European competition. Next year, once again, getting to the quarter-finals of a World Cup will be the best we can hope for, yet still we tell ourselves we have the best team in the world. OK, Sky tells us, and we believe it. Just as we believe we are the most tolerant country, the most polite, the most phlegmatic, with the best sense of humour, all of which is brainwashed bollocks.

Brazil, Argentina, France and Italy are miles better. Greece and Portugal have recently done better. Holland and Germany—remember, the Germans will be playing at home—will rise to the occasion. Either Ghana, Japan or Korea, or another South American team, will surprise us all, and England might not even make the last 16. And all thanks to Sven. Oh yes, I'll be blaming him.

We do have, by chance, a handful of world-class individuals at this moment, such as Wayne Rooney, Steven Gerrard, Frank Lampard, John Terry, Rio Ferdinand and David Beckham, players acknowledged by the rest of the world. Most England fans are quite happy with all 11 players Sven usually picks, because he tends to go for the best, most obvious choices available at any one moment. That's his first mistake. The 11 best players don't make the best team. Thus, we end up with too many doing a similar job in midfield, cancelling each other out.

Alf Ramsey didn't pick the best 11 in the summer of 1966, otherwise Jimmy Greaves would always have been in. Nobody thought Nobby Stiles was world-class or Martin Peters worth his place. A team manager has to manage to create a team, fit different players together, even if it makes him unpopular, in order to make the whole better than the sum of its parts. Then he has to form a strategy. So far, Sven has proved useless at both. And when the individuals are patently doing badly, he freezes, doesn't know how to change it.

I can see no point in having him as manager. Most fans could do what he does. It's giving me a headache, just thinking of his England team. I'll just check out the cricket. Oh, good ball, Shaney; well played, Vaughney; Flintoffy, you're fantasticky.

Cricketers are the most beautifully dressed sportsmen. Or so the wife says

12 September 2005

WHO ARE THE LOVELIEST OF THEM ALL? MY WIFE has no doubt whatsoever. She came into my room today, before I had a chance to switch off the cricket, because of course I hate cricket, not interested, game for nancies and poshos. I'd only been watching it for two hours, perhaps three—OK, the best part of the day, just because I couldn't find any footer.

"Oooh," she said, or sounds to that effect. "I do think cricketers are the world's best-dressed sportsmen." Don't drool over me, pet. Get back in that kitchen and clean those pots.

First of all, she loves their long white trousers, so attractive, and their sleeveless cable-knit white pullies. Then when they put on their visors she imagines them as knights in armour. Racing drivers: she also likes their outfits, especially their white boiler suits, zipped up to the neck, like something out of Casualty. Skiers, in their jackets and skin-tight trousers, they look good, and of course jockeys have always worn pretty clothes, but overall, cricketers are the most beautifully dressed. That's her considered opinion.

I was rather insulted, especially because she said footballers are about the worst looking. "No sportsman should wear shorts." I happen to have been in shorts since May, and intend to carry on until October, when we return to London, even if it does snow.

The only shorts-wearing sportsmen she had a good word for were the New Zealand All Blacks. Wearing all black is in itself attractive, fashion-wise, but they also do fill their shirts and shorts so well, having, ahem, such excellent physiques.

That is *sooo* lookist, which we in football never worry about, otherwise Lee Bowyer, Paul Scholes and Shaun Wright-Phillips would never get in the dressing room, never mind on the pitch. Not exactly hunks, are they? It's one of the many reasons football is a world game. Anybody can play it.

When I look at footballers, dressed for football, I don't look at their bodies. I am looking at history, thinking of the long, proud traditions of the club colours they are carrying, of fans who have been shouting "Come on you Reds", or similar, for more than a hundred years now. As a schoolboy, I could tell you the strip of all 92 League clubs, plus Scotland. On the whole, the colours and designs have stayed roughly the same, despite all the nasty commercial logos.

OK, apart from Arsenal. I quite like their new redcurrant shirt, from an aesthetic point of view, but if I were an Arsenal fan, I would be upset by the loss of their traditional strip. Though in fact it dates back only to the 1930s, when their manager Herbert Chapman introduced the white sleeves to make them more distinctive. Their shirts had been all red before that, a design they pinched from Nottingham Forest.

In England, you don't get green shirts, one exception being Plymouth Argyle. In England, the founding fathers considered green unlucky. Why was this? Theories, please. In Scotland, it didn't bother Celtic or Hibs.

The luckiest colour is red, according to my latest copy of *Durham First*, the university's alumni mag. Two academics in the department of anthropology examined athletes in the 2004 Olympics who were competing in one-on-one disciplines, such as boxing and wrestling, where competitors were randomly assigned red or blue clothing. Those wearing red, so they discovered, were more likely to win. Fascinating, huh?

In the very early days, before it all settled down, clubs did mess around with their strips. I have an 1876 photo of Hearts, now doing so well in Scotland, looking very ducky in white shirts with a heart on their left breast. In 1884, Bolton Wanderers were wearing white shirts with red spots, which were said to make them look bigger. That same year, they appeared in a cup match wearing salmon pink — playing Notts County, who were in chocolate and blue. Good enough to eat.

Cricketers, eh? Their play might be exciting at present, but I think they look boring in all white. Shows no imagination.

No more foreigners, please — from now on, our footie will be strictly British

19 September 2005

WOULDN'T IT BE LUVVERLY IF WHAT SEPP BLATTER is recommending comes to pass. He's President of Fifa and is normally viewed as a total wally by most of the football world, but for once, the initial reaction of most fans has been to say "yeessss". He wants professional clubs to restrict the number of foreign players. At the moment, there are no rules about this in Britain, which means that such clubs as Chelsea or Arsenal can and have had on the field 11 foreign-born players.

They kiss their badges, say they are so proud to play for the Blues/Reds, love their long tradition, the best fans in the world, tra la, all of which is total nonsense, not to say a bloomin' porky. 'Scuse me, this word porky, you eat it, yah? And bloomin', is not in my dictionary?

When we cheer on Portsmouth or Bolton Wanderers, wouldn't it be nice to think that most players have some connection with the place, or at least could make a reasonable stab at finding it on the map? Unlikely today. Portsmouth has 17 different nationalities in its first-team squad while Bolton has 16. On the first day of this season, the starting line-ups in the Premiership contained 86 English-born players, compared with 103 foreigners. For those taking notes, the foreigners came from: France, Holland and the Republic of Ireland — 12 each; Spain and Denmark — nine each; Scotland — eight; Wales — seven; Northern Ireland, Australia, Nigeria and Finland — four each; Sweden and the United States — three each; Colombia, Cote d'Ivoire, Germany, Iceland, Israel and Portugal — two each.

Blatter's argument is that having so many foreigners over here, filling our team sheets, taking our money, shagging our women, deprives Brit-born lads. Brits might get into a Premiership academy, but their chances of making the first team are zilch. Poom. I forgot him. Comes from Estonia. Add him to the list.

This would appear very bad for football generally and Britain in particular. But is it? A Premiership academy might not get you into a Premiership team, but you still have a chance of making a career lower down the British leagues, or abroad.

And, whatever happens, the pool of professional players across the whole world, assuming we still have the same number of clubs, will remain the same. It will just mean more will have to stay in their own country. At present, while relatively few of our home-grown lads have a chance to be on a million a year and have all the women they can wear, it is giving a chance for lads from Cote d'Ivoire or Nigeria to win fame and fortune over here, and improve their football, which they could never have managed, staying at home. Isn't that fair? Isn't that good for world football?

Ah, but the romance will go out of football, if every player in your local team is foreign. In the end, the fans won't stand for it. Not true, either. The mind and emotions of a fan are very strange. He is capable of turning anyone from anywhere into a Scouser or Geordie overnight.

Arsenal fans really did consider "Paddy" Vieira one of them, a true born Gooner, until he did a runner. Chelsea fans voted that little Italian Zola their best ever player. Just after the war, when we still looked upon all Jerries as baddies, Bert Trautmann, a German ex-POW, became one of Man City's all-time heroes. He helped them win the FA Cup, despite a broken neck. Typical British bulldog spirit, eh?

The truth is, fans don't care about your birthplace or what language you speak—only if you can play well. And it's always been that way, from the very beginning. I often ask people to guess how many players in the Spurs team that won the FA Cup in 1901 actually came from London. Go on, try it. The answer is none: five were Scots, two were Welsh and one was Irish, while the three Englishmen came from Maryport, the Potteries and Grantham.

So sorry, Sepp. Footballers have always been mercenaries. You can't change that now. Me, I think that, if there is going to be a law limiting foreigners, it should apply just to managers. And only to England managers. In fact, just one country. No more Swedes, please.

When Saturday comes, the lady wife becomes my best friend

26 September 2005

I'VE GOT ONE PROBLEM THIS SEASON ABOUT GOING to watch Carlisle United. It's 40 miles away from our house in Loweswater as the sheep fly, which I normally can do easily, pleasantly, in less than an hour, taking the scenic route over the Caldbeck Fells. It's so pretty yet so empty, one of the nicest drives anywhere in Cumbria. The problem is, I can't drive.

No need to go into all the reasons, you'd just be interested, but it's not due to drunken driving. I had a violent seizure in June after my younger daughter's wedding in France. It hasn't happened again, but if you have it once, that's it—you lose your licence for a year.

I'll be your best friend, I said to the wife, Your Majesty, Your Wonderfulness, if only you'll drive me to Carlisle. Yes, I know it's a Saturday. You wouldn't believe the crowds and traffic. Le toot Cumbria pours in, if only to stand on the pavements and look at the shop windows. Rural people don't get a lot of excitement.

She can drive, having passed her test ten years ago in Cockermouth, but has never driven since. Hates driving, hates my car. Gradually, she has begun driving the seven miles into Cockermouth once a week for the shopping. Done very well. All I have to do is ring the police and they clear the road. Joke. Which I'll have to stop making as it's very patronising, and won't help me get to Carlisle.

But she agreed to take me, as she too loves the scenic route, setting off early doors so we'd find parking. It was so strange driving down Warwick Road to Brunton Park. Almost every house had a skip outside and most ground-floor windows and doors were boarded up. Had a bomb gone off? A hurricane struck? I'd forgotten the huge floods Carlisle suffered back in January. The city is still cleaning itself up, and many remain homeless.

Brunton Park itself, which used to boast the best playing surface of any ground in the Football League, was totally flooded, with the water at one stage higher than the cross-bars. You're winding me up, I said to David Clark, one of the directors, as I looked out at the perfectly pristine pitch. He's a Labour life peer, ex-cabinet minister, so he wouldn't lie, would he, or even exaggerate.

The club, very wisely, had excellent insurance covering itself for loss of home gates, not just damage. Unlike some of the surrounding householders, Carlisle were able to make repairs remarkably quickly. In fact, the club exudes an air of quiet prosperity, with all the refurbished offices, a sparkling new carpet in the directors' lounge and a handsome new statue of Hugh McIlmoyle outside the ground. You probably haven't heard of him if you live south of Penrith, but he's a legend the length of Warwick Road.

It is as if last season, when Carlisle made the dreaded drop to the Conference League, somehow revitalised them.

Now they are back up again, they seem invigorated. On my visit, they were playing Barnet, who ran away with the Conference title last year, but Carlisle dominated the first half and were one up. Second half, hmm, it all went wonky, and Barnet got three simple goals.

Afterwards I talked to the club's owner and saviour, Fred Story, a local builder. He was blaming a certain player, whom he says he can't stand. "Oh, the manager knows my feelings. I've told him." And what does he say in reply? "He makes no comment. He knows anyway I would never interfere, but I am allowed my opinion."

And yet the crowd did not seem too downhearted, convinced that CUFC was the better team. Which has turned out true, as Carlisle have now zoomed up the League and could well get promoted.

Most of the directors were happy, too, when I joined them later for a drink. Or three. Come on, I was a guest. And I wasn't driving, so I could enjoy myself. There are some advantages to losing your licence.

Now the Premiership clubs will have to be nice to all of us, all the time

3 October 2005

IT'S EXCELLENT NEWS ABOUT THE PREMIER LEAGUE. So pleased that gates are dropping, hee hee hee, and that the clubs are having a special meeting in a few weeks to explore the reasons and try to attract the fans back, har har har. God, I can hardly contain myself.

I've been chuntering on about this for three years, pointing up the signs, warning what would happen if we continued to be ripped off and treated like dirt. Shit has hit the fans. Now the fans are hitting back.

Reasons to be glad:

- On my return to London and the Premiership, it'll be so comfy. When the midfield pass the ball around aimlessly, going further and further backwards till they pass to the goalie, I'll be able to stretch out and have a snooze, thanks to the empty seats either side.
- Kids and grandads and dogs were always able to turn up at any training ground and watch their heroes. That stopped with the Premiership. Clubs became so rich and self-important that they banned such access, erecting security gates, putting tanks at all corners, shoot to kill if

any kid looked through the barbed wire. Now they'll have to be nice to all fans, all the time.

• Prem players, since becoming millionaires, never venture out without ten armed guards. Ask for an autograph, and one of the heavies takes you to a corner and duffs you up. Now all players will have to sign when asked, even by dogs.

• Players' wives have been able to have designer stores closed when they shop and beaches cleared when taking their tops off. Now they'll have to queue at Wilkinson's like the rest of us.

• Fergie will be forced to give a post-match media interview, every time, including all hospital radio stations and every parish mag that asks.

• Ford Focus salesmen will be over the moon as players dump their Ferraris in the street, unable to afford the petrol.

• Clubs will copy Waterstone's and offer three for two. Anyone, such as me, who is foolish enough to pay a fortune to both Spurs and Arsenal will get a Chelsea season ticket thrown in for free. In Cumbria, buy one for Carlisle United and Workington, and you'll also get Gretna. What a bargain. They are top of their division (Scottish Second, just to save you looking).

• Players, having to struggle on only a million a year, get testimonials, mostly for doing bugger all, apart from taking the money. Now fans will get testimonials. After ten years' devotion, the club will organise a celebrity raffle, a black-tie ball and a friendly against Real Madrid—and you will keep all the money.

• All programmes will be free, as they mostly are in Spain

and Italy. Here they cost £3, and are full of adverts or arse licks for sponsors.

- Prem clubs, when they cost-cut, will send home some of their expensive foreigners, which means we'll have teams with at least one player born locally ... OK, let's say within 300 miles.
- No more first-team squads of 156, or enough in the case of Chelsea for three first elevens in any other league. It's such a waste seeing human beings at the top of their careers warming their butts on a bench. Oh so sad.
- All clubs will lay on free buses from every point in town to take you to the ground and back. No more need for the hell of parking, which, I think, is one of the main reasons fans have stopped going.
- Every game to start at three o'clock on a Saturday. That's another reason fans have got pissed off. Who wants to travel right across the country, or even drag themselves to their local ground, at some stupid time on a freezing Monday evening in winter, when it's all on the telly anyway?
- Fewer games on Sky.

Actually, delete that last one. My personal philosophy of life is that you can't be too rich, have too many corkscrews or have too many live games on telly.

Apart from that, I can honestly see nothing but good coming out of this shock-horror crisis for the Premiership, ho ho ho.

In Becks Major's book, Sven will find all the tips he needs to manage England

10 October 2005

THAT GREAT UPMARKET, INTELLECTUAL, TOP QUALITY newspaper, *The Times*, has been serialising the biography of one of the most important and influential figures in world football — Ted Beckham. Fans everywhere will always be indebted to him for siring young David.

There was intense competition for the serial rights, notably a last-minute bid from *The Beano*, which reportedly offered a "high four-figure sum" (thought to be £19.99). If only it had got "into bed" with the *Dandy* (this is a technical expression oft used in newspaper and magazine bidding wars, and not in any way associated with Boy David), it might have pulled it off.

Just as well for me. *The Beano* and *Dandy* are late arriving up here in Lakeland — I think the postie reads them first. But one of my gardeners gets *The Times*, so I was able to devour every word of *David Beckham: my son by Ted Beckham*. The price is £18.99, but *The Times* is doing a special offer, post free, at £17.09. That's all my Christmas presents settled.

Among the pearls, the paragraph that struck me most was the exclusive revelation that David sucked a dummy until he was six. He'd probably be sucking it to this day, so Ted reveals, but for some smart work by David's mother, Sandra.

"Sandra decided that he had to give it up. She told him it was time for our pet rabbit to have it—a ruse of course—and she was expecting a big fuss. But next day, he dropped the dummy into the hutch and that was the end of it."

Brilliant! I have two grandchildren, one of whom is six, and I'm sure each was well aware by the age of two, perhaps three max, that rabbits don't in fact use a dummy. But of course my grandchildren are incredibly advanced and this is 2005. Dad Becks is describing a scene that took place in suburban Essex back in the dark days of the early Eighties. Understandable.

I do hope Sven has read and digested every word. It could help him, in whatever he is doing now, wherever he may be.

I have to cover myself in case by the time you read this we've been stuffed by Austria and Poland, and Sven has resigned in a hissy but silent fit and is now in the wastes of Arctic Sweden, with only his millions to keep him warm.

Two things have always puzzled me about his style of management, which otherwise has been exemplary, not to say excellent. First, he never makes notes. Now this is unusual in modern management. It could of course be that his brain is so big, his memory so phenomenal. And yet most top foreign managers, such as José Mourinho and

Rafael Benitez, do make notes during a game, as do young English pretenders such as Alan Curbishley and Alan Pardew. It always heartens me to watch them, scribbling away in the dugout. I feel cheered, pleased, nay proud. Writing is not dead, I tell myself; there is still a place for it in this technological age, despite iPods, whatever they are, and miniature mobile phones. I am glad for my successors in the field of football biography, hacks to come, who will have something concrete to go on: thoughts of great men preserved for ever, for I'm sure modern managers never throw such precious items away. They have to think of the royalties to come.

Second, Sven always leaves ten minutes before the end of every game. I always presumed it was to avoid the traffic, as of course he is a very important person, with at least six teams a year to pick, and only one pencil. Or he's simply hurrying home to Nancy, or similar. But last weekend, at Charlton for their game against Spurs, there he was, well before the end, gone. Yet we know Charlton get small gates, so there was no need to rush. So why had he done a bunk, early doors?

Obviously, to finish off Becks Major's book. And in it, he will have found all the aide-memoires, notes and tips he'll ever need to manage England. For surely the reason England were able to hammer Austria and Poland was that, at half-time, Sven gave David a dummy to calm him down/the reason we got thumped was that Sven forgot David's dummy. (Note to editor: please delete whichever is not applicable. Thanks.)

Anyone wise, sensible and quietly superior wouldn't respond. But I will

17 October 2005

I GOT A BIT UPSET LAST WEEK, READING SOMEONE ranting against football fans, saying they were lumpen, stupid, boring, why didn't they get a life, while the players were vacuous and the media craven in devoting so much time to football. All of it spot on—have I not been saying it for years? So what's the problem, Hunt?

Just that I don't like it coming from someone who admits to not being a football fan. It's like someone outside the family rubbishing your wife, your kids, your house, your curtains, your tortoise. You can do it. They can't.

Anyone sure of themselves, their family, or their love for football, would naturally not respond, being wise, sensible and, of course, quietly superior. Being none of the above, I did find myself thinking about it for the rest of the day. Lost the article now. Oh yeah, it was in that excellent mag, the *New Statesman*. By Andrew Martin. Good piece, son.

But we've heard it all before, and much worse, right back to 1888, when an English professional league was first formed. That was football ruined, spoiled for ever, cried all the public-school amateurs; fair play, honesty and honour, that's gone for ever. Football has become corrupt, so they all moaned. And it's still true. Players lie and cheat, if they think they can get away with it, say it's their throw-in when they know it's not, claim false penalties, con the ref, try to injure rival players.

Football clubs themselves are corrupt. It began with pound notes in your boots after a game, at a time when any payments were illegal. Gate receipts were fiddles, cash creamed off to pay backhanders to seduce away rival stars. Today, the whole process of agents and transfers and bogus middlemen taking a share, along with some managers or their relations, is totally tainted. We all know that, we fans, yawn yawn.

Players' wages and transfers are said to be obscene today. And yesterday. In 1905, Alf Common was transferred from Sunderland to Middlesbrough for the then incredible sum of £1,000. We now have white slavery, said the back pages, players have become mercenaries, football will never be the same again, sob sob. Which, of course, was deadly inaccurate.

The fans, they are indeed stupid lumps, aren't they? Always have been. I have in front of me an article in the *Graphic* of 29 April 1911, in which Sir Philip Gibbs bewails the behaviour of Cup Final fans he has just witnessed. "A horde of barbarians invaded London on Saturday, many with big fists and brawny shoulders, hard and dour in the mould of their faces, not softness, nor grace, nor elegance ... like sheer savages, they went stupidly about. It is rather awful to think that these loafers who invaded London have become decadent before becoming civilised."

God, he was enjoying himself, but he would have had

more fun today, and produced even purpler prose, on realising that most fans have got decent jobs, that they work hard, have nice homes to go to, thin shoulders and slender fists, and that some can speak Latin. And they are bloody well-off. Have to be. Otherwise how could any of them afford £70 for a half-decent seat at Spurs?

Football, the game, is stupid. Twenty-two grown men with bare legs chasing a ball around a piece of grass—what's the point in that? None at all. It's not politics, or economics, war or peace, none of them serious things, know what I mean?

I must be utterly demented, pathetic, everything lacking in my life, to have watched three Premiership games live on TV the other Sunday, one after the other. Daft or what? And yet I can get so elated by a good game, even a good move, can see elegance and grace in footballers and in the fans, where Gibbs could see none. I get depressed by a bad game, yet find myself looking forward, yearning, to the next. Football does enrich my life. I smile in anticipation of the World Cup.

But I don't see all this as a winning game. I never say football is better than cricket, that cricket is slow and boring (even though it is). I just like football. I do think it is a beautiful game.

Good job I was wearing sun specs in the car park at White Hart Lane

24 October 2005

QUITE A CONTRAST WITH BRUNTON PARK AND Carlisle United, going to my first Premiership game of the season. In the flesh, or what's left of it. For a start, the car park at White Hart Lane. Good job I was wearing sun specs. The razzle-dazzle, the flashing dashing opulence of the grossly over-the-top, conspicuously expenditured motors could have ruined my eyesight. Never seen so many Ferraris, Aston Martins and Bentleys parked in one small space. Boys aged about ten were standing gaping. I think some never actually took their seats for the game, preferring to ogle the car porn.

Compared with last season, there were also a lot more gigantic 4x4 models, designer specials, by the look of them. One was so huge it would have been more at home in Main Street, Basra, than High Road, Tottenham. I was told it was a director's, not a player's. But how would a player know? They have so many.

I've been back in London only a week, and travelling on the bus quite a few times, I noticed what everyone notices about London — the enormous cultural and ethnic mix. But not at Spurs. I didn't see a black or Asian face among the crowds on the way to the game, nor did I hear a posho middle-class accent. They could, of course, have been crouching. It was a heaving mass of white, pasty norf London faces and voices, and most of them were stuffing their gobs when not on their mobiles.

Inside, there's been an addition to the names and slogans on the hoarding behind the Park Lane goals. For about a hundred years, they've been content to leave the Spurs club motto, "Audere est Facere", in its original Latin, which we all used to speak, in the days when football began. "Oh dear, it's fucked," is what I've always taken it to mean. I do have O-level Latin.

Now they've stuck up a literal translation, in large letters: "To dare is to do." The words just stand there, on their own, not making much sense, unless it's the precursor of another advertising campaign. In the act of being daring, you are obviously doing something, ain'tcha? So what's the point of saying it? Unless it means that you succeed by daring. In other words, "Who dares, wins." But that's been well used.

Poncy, awful, orchestral mush music heralded the teams coming out, which I gather has been ordained by Sky TV for all Premiership games, but then later we did get "Glory, glory, Tot-nam Hotspur" and then at half-time, "McNamara's Band".

The fans are still singing that rude song about Sol Campbell, which ends in "up my arse", but they have now adapted "Yellow Submarine" for home consumption. For about five years now I have heard European crowds singing this tune, without knowing what words they were using. I was interested that Europeans not English fans should have adopted it first.

The words used by the Spurs fans are all very clean, so you can read on without fear of blushing. "Num-ber One is Rob-bee Keane, Rob-bee Keane, Rob-bee Keane/Number Two is Rob-bee Keane, Rob-bee Keane, Rob-bee Keane ..." And so on, up to Number 12, if they've got the energy, or unless something exciting happens. Finally, they sing. "We all foll-ow the Robbie Keane team, the Robbie Keane team." Catchy, huh.

Yeah, of course, I was there for the football, not social and cultural observation, and Spurs were excellent, stuffing poor old Everton two-nil. Spurs now have 43 midfield players, most of whom look alike, and play alike, except for Edgar Davids, who is by far the best. All these years, watching him on TV, I never realised how small he is. And relatively weedy. That was a surprise. Ah, you can't beat football in the flesh.

I longed to be a football reporter, but today's spoilt stars must make it hell

31 October 2005

IN OCTOBER 1958, AGED 22, I JOINED THE STAFF OF the Manchester Evening Chronicle as a graduate trainee journalist. It was nine months after the Munich air crash, in which eight football journalists had died, along with the Manchester United victims.

My heroes on the paper were Keith Dewhurst and Ray Wergan, who respectively covered Man Utd and Man City. They wore white raincoats with the collar turned up, got acres in the papers, knew all the players. Oh, how I longed to be a football reporter.

I never actually became one. While on *The Sunday Times*, in the 1960s, I was in other departments, though I occasionally offered to do a match report if they wanted something silly. In the 1970s, while working on a football book, I covered some games more seriously, to pick up background material.

I often think, if times get hard with books and I'm demoted to publishers from the Third Division (North), I might try football reporting again. Then I think nah, must be hell today, with these spoilt multi-millionaires up their own arses, surrounded by agents, lawyers, security guards.

I bet they treat national reporters like vermin and don't even realise local hacks exist.

Dan Carrier is 32, went to Sussex University and covers Spurs for the *Camden New Journal,* where he's also news editor. It's a free paper, a breed journalists normally look down on, but a good one, recently winning the Free Newspaper of the Year award. So, Dan, you must get treated like shit by a big club like Spurs? "Not at all. I think I get better treatment than the nationals. The press office return my calls more quickly, because they know I won't be stirring up trouble.

"I started covering Spurs five years ago, so I've watched young players develop. Stephen Kelly, for example, will always talk to me. He's just so excited to have got in the squad. The foreign players are usually good as well. Steffen Freund once gave me tickets for the players' lounge, which he wouldn't do for a tabloid. Today, Edgar Davids is very helpful. The only problem is his voice is so low I can hardly hear him. Mido arrived with a reputation for being moody and difficult, but I think he's on a charm offensive, trying to make a good impression."

Foreign players, of course, don't know which are the big by-line tabloid stars and which are the local hacks, and this helps people like Dan. Officially, they all get the same facilities—press box, press lounge, steak pie at half-time, seat at the manager's press conference afterwards, able to ask any questions. But with the players themselves, the system is as it always was—all newspaper hacks have to hang around the car park, outside the players' entrance, hoping for a quick word.

The present-day stars of Spurs, such as Defoe or Keane, won't say much to anyone if they've had a poor game. "I often feel sorry for them," says Dan, "Having to put up with us asking the same old questions, then I think, hang on, they're on 60 grand a week."

Being so wealthy has in some ways equalled things out. At one time, players kept in with the tabloids, hoping for a fee or a ghosted column. Now they're mega-rich, they can be nice or not nice to all hacks, regardless.

Dan usually manages at least six seconds of exclusive chat with manager Martin Jol. "He's got a wicked sense of humour. Hoddle was helpful, but he spoke in clichés or babble, which made the going hard for me, as I try to get three pieces about Spurs in each issue."

He has mobile numbers for ten of the first-team squad but uses them sparingly, clearing his queries with the press office first. He knows not to abuse his access. But he never would. Like many local-born, local paper reporters, he's a diehard fan of his local team.

"I've even been known to ask Martin Jol to sign my programme. Yeah, I know, very unprofessional. The press box at Spurs is just behind the bench. I have this fantasy that I'm actually a player. And that one day I'll be called on ..."

Ah, takes me back. I had that fantasy once, till my poorly knee.

Yes, Premiership football is watched all over the world —by the Brits

7 November 2005

PATHETIC, REALLY, GOING ALL THAT WAY, SPENDING all that money to stay at the wonderful Elounda Beach Hotel, the sun shining on the blue Mediterranean outside, and there we were last week, sitting inside, watching Man Utd *v* Spurs on the telly in a bar. Later, on the way back from Crete, I did my usual family quiz, asking everyone to give marks out of five for the best meal, best thing. My son put watching Spurs in that bar in his top three things. I didn't go that far. I do have standards. But it made my top five.

I was distracted, while watching the game, by all the British football shirts hanging on every wall. I counted 200, each carefully mounted to display the front. I spotted Carlisle Utd's, miles out of date, the Eddie Stobart deckchair one they haven't worn for years, but at least CUFC was represented. I wondered how the owner had managed to get a shirt from every British club. They cost at least £35 these days, which comes to £7,000 worth. I suppose he gets it back by filling his bar with pathetic Brit fans on their hols.

When we first entered the bar, the three monster TV screens, each the size of my house, were showing a Greek game, a German game, plus Spurs. The owner soon sussed out the nature of the audience who happened to have wandered in that day and switched all three screens to Spurs. Oh bliss.

They always boast that the Premier League is watched all over the world, which from my awfully long experience of the globe, is true. I don't think I've failed to discover some English football somewhere on local TV. They then boast it's therefore the world's most popular league. Foreign fans love its speed, energy, excitement, crowds, blah blah. I think that's not true. From my long experience, etc, it's Brits abroad, in bars and hotels, who are mainly watching it, pathetic creatures that we are.

I was once on my hols in Turkey. The TV lounge was absolutely chocka for a local Turkish game, standing room only, all the Turks screaming and shouting. After it came the English Cup Final, which was what I'd come to watch, beamed to 550 different countries, plus Mars, so we are told every year. The room immediately emptied. I watched it on my own.

In that Elounda harbour-side bar, there were only about 20 people, quietly watching, all of whom I took to be Brits. Judging by their reactions, almost all were Spurs fans. It was the last week of October, the end of Crete's tourist season. In the hotels, bars, taxis, they'd been working for seven months, non-stop, seven days a week. Now they were about to close for five months. They get some unemployment pay from the government over the winter, when they are not picking olives or doing a bit of fishing, till the cycle starts again.

It had been a good season, so all the locals said, and people in the tourist business rarely admit that. They put it down to the Olympics and Greece winning the Euro Nations Championship, two events which had put the country on the map, creating a knock-on effect.

Now, there was an end-of-season feeling, the crowds gone, the staff relaxed, life slowing down. The handful of Spurs fans were being treated to endless plates of crisps and nuts, hoping we'd stay all evening, if not all week.

At half-time, I worked out who the owner was and asked him how much he paid, and to whom, for the TV rights. They show all Sky games live, even ones we don't see in Britain till much later. That can happen in Britain, but is usually done illegally. He wouldn't tell me how much, but he said it was beamed in via another country and was quite expensive.

I then asked about his shirts. Had he gone to the UK and bought them personally, or got them mail order? Neither. Apart from two, they had all been given. Fans visit his bar, look around for their team's strip. If they don't see it, they strip off and donate the one they are wearing. If by some oversight they have gone on holiday not wearing their team's shirt, tut tut, they donate one the following year, coming back specially. Now is that also pathetic? Course not. It's pride, innit.

My unused ticket to last week's game could yet be part of my pension

14 November 2005

I HAVE THIS HALF SEASON FOR ARSENAL, HAVE DONE for a long time. I just follow the Arse. No, the deal is I only watch half of every game, leaving at half-time so someone else can take my seat. Joke. OK, what I do is sit there all the time, but I can only watch one half of the pitch. I have to close my eyes when the ball goes in the other half. Another joke.

Obviously, what I do is have it for half of the season, subletting it from an Arsenal friend. He has three season tickets, one notionally for his son, but he is working abroad at present. My half has just begun, in time to see Arsenal against Sparta Prague in the Euro Champions League. Good timing, because you get these early Euro games for free, in the sense that it comes with your season ticket.

But not so good in that it was a Wednesday evening, pouring down and it was live on the telly. Two hours before the game, my friend rang to say he had another ticket going spare, and did I know anyone who could use it?

I try to keep it quiet locally that I have a half Arsenal ticket because I'm supposedly a Spurs fan. Which I am, oh yes. But first I'm a football fan. I just like to see a good game. I rang a couple of neighbours whom I know to be Arsenal fans and they said: "Wotyoudoinwifanarsnalticket?" But both were going to watch it in the pub. In the end, the ticket was not used. Isn't that awful, a notional £50 totally wasted—except it wasn't. I have it here in front of me, pristine and whole. My friend gave it to me; as he said, it's of no use to him.

One of the strange things in football memorabilia in the past five years is the rise of tickets. Programmes have been kept, and treasured, since at least the 1870s when they first appeared, little more than a card, with the teams on one side and perhaps a couple of adverts on the reverse. By the 1900s, they had grown much bigger, up to 20 pages, with lots of fascinating facts, figures, articles and illustrations. I can spend hours reading my old programmes. Well, I have got a poorly knee. Good and interesting old programmes can now change hands for up to £15,000. Tickets, on the other hand, are totally boring, content-wise, as there's nothing to read. They're not even of interest typographically, as the same old layout goes on for decades. Until recently, they were worthless. Football fans just threw them away.

Now they have suddenly started to appear in catalogues and sales. I kept my own ticket for the 1966 World Cup final, for the simple reason that I throw nothing away. It's now worth £150. Amazing. Pre-war cup final tickets go for £300, according to the latest catalogue from the country's largest football programme dealer, Sports Programmes of Bedfordshire. By tickets, I mean stubs—because, of course, a bit gets taken off when you go through the turnstile. But my Arsenal-Sparta Prague ticket is unused and complete. It could be part of my pension.

The match, I nearly forgot, yeah, it was good. Arsenal won 3–0. What else?

There's a new sign up in Highbury that says "Kings of London", which must piss off Chelsea. And just to rub it in, the Arsenal crowd, when bored, start chanting: "Fuck off Mourinho."

Thierry Henry has a new trick. A season ago he had this habit of doing a sort of half turn with the ball, with his back to his opponent, which when it worked looked dead clever. This season he's working on a step-over to the side, as if he's going round a player with the ball, but in fact he has left it behind, stationary. The trouble is that he tends to get clattered by the lumpen opponent before he can retrieve it.

Henry, now he's captain, has got it into his head that he must clap whenever any Arsenal player gives a remotely half-decent ball, pour encourager les lads, even when a player is 100 yards away. It means he spends half his time with his hands up in the air.

Robin van Persie, now he looks really good, taller than I had imagined. When Bergkamp finally packs it in, Persie could be just the ticket.

I take it all back — we are so lucky having Sven, and so cheaply

21 November 2005

I WAS WALKING BACK ACROSS HAMPSTEAD HEATH when I saw two young schoolgirls, aged about 14, coming towards me, laughing and shouting, arms around each other, all very harmless, all very normal for that time of day, it being coming-out-of-school time. They were from Parliament Hill School, which one of my daughters used to attend, though I didn't know either of these girls. Not that I was taking much notice.

As they approached, one of them stopped and smiled at me. "I like your walking stick," she said. "It's very fashionable." I've got this poorly knee, having had a total knee replacement seven months ago which I wish I'd never had, what a mistake, don't get me started. My stick is more of a prop really, but it is rather smart, sort of black cane. And it's collapsible, which you wouldn't realise, looking at it. It folds into five sections. I got it at Firn's in Cockermouth, only £14. Mail order, they're much more expensive.

"Thank you," I said to the girl.

For a moment, I thought, "I'll demonstrate its wonders, collapse it in front of them, won't they be amazed, then snap it straight again." That always amuses my two granddaughters, aged five and six. Then I thought, "No, could look a bit pathetic, trying to impress 14-year-olds."

Both girls smiled, started to walk on, until they were right beside me. The other girl suddenly stopped, held out her arms towards me. "Would you like a hug?" I was totally taken aback. Into my head came the front page of next week's *Camden New Journal*: "Old git in sixties accosts 14-year-old schoolgirls". Nobody, in this present age, would ever believe my version. "Er, how kind, but er, no thanks," I said, walking on hurriedly. When I got home I told my wife. She gave me a funny look. "I think they were being satirical," she said.

"Don't be daft," I said. "It's part of the national euphoria". I'd noticed that one of them was wearing an England T-shirt, obviously still carried away by the general air of rejoicing. Our lads winning does perk us all up. I myself have felt a warm glow all week, but I didn't manage to get to any of the street parties—a bit too cold, and there's my poorly knee. But I bet all shops will now have a record Xmas, shares will rise, and Tony Blair will win any vote he wants. Gordon Brown will smile, even though none of the England team plays for East Fife. Or is his team Raith Rovers? I've got confused with all the excitement.

Having already won the World Cup, Sven deserves his four-month break. I clearly saw him standing up. Totally brilliant. And he once even went to the touchline. Now that was a master stroke.

After that 3–2 win over Argentina, I take back anything nasty I ever said about him. We are so lucky having him, and so cheaply. It's an insult to his brilliance, paying him only £4m a year. Rooney of course is a genius. So is Wee Michael. Ditto Becks. In fact, we have a team full of geniuses. Gawd, we are so fortunate, living in these times.

Yes, the guys got in each other's way now and again, and the Argies did rather carve us up in the first half-hour, but hey, they are a good team. But not as good as us. Nobody is. Little wonder that Brazil, Germany, Italy, France have all backed out of going to Germany, scared shitless by the very thought of Rooney and Owen. I read that in the *Sun*, or was it the *Mirror*? But of course it would be pointless them going anyway, as we've already won.

I'll treasure for ever that image of Becks holding aloft the 2006 World Cup in Geneva after that amazing win, which John Motson described so graphically. That was the final, wasn't it? I'm sure that's what Motty said. I've tried to contact him, but he experienced so many orgasms during that game that he's been lying down in a dark room ever since. Well, he is an old gent in his sixties. He shouldn't get so excited, but it is very easy to get carried away, misunderstand the signals. I've sent him my stick. It might help him to get around, once he returns to normal life.

Alas, Roy Keane was a thug, and thugs in football are an endangered species

28 November 2005

SO ROY KEANE HAS GONE FROM OLD TRAFFORD, NO longer Man United's captain and motivating force, inspiration and leader, greatest ever midfield player, a living legend, totally irreplaceable, oh do get on with it. Yes, an era has passed, Brian, they don't make them like that any more, we will not see his like again, and other bollocks. Thank Gawd for that.

Because he was a thug, and thugs in football, so I suspect and honestly hope, are an endangered species. At one time, every team had at least one player whose speciality was thuggishness, whose job it was to snuff out, duff up, put the frighteners on, use any physical means to make sure the opposition's star creative player did not create and, with a bit of luck, did not even get a chance to play.

Defenders may be rough and tough, clumsy and lumpen, may flatten and upend, but on the whole they are not thugs, even though their main job is to stop, to negate. Generally they wait, ready to react, rather than go out looking for trouble. It's mostly a midfield player who gets given the specific, destructive job, and often given a specific man to destroy. Norman Hunter of Leeds used to bite legs.

Tommy Smith of Liverpool ate razor blades and half a cow for breakfast. Nobby Stiles of Man United, despite being thin and weedy, kicked anything human that dared move. "Chopper" Harris of Chelsea chopped bodies into little pieces, then spat them out, looking innocent.

More recently, Vinnie Jones of Wimbledon was a master of the black arts, verbal, emotional and physical. That infamous incident when he grabbed Gazza by the balls, caught on photograph, occurred in 1987, when Gazza was young and fresh in the Newcastle team. The minute they kicked off, Vinnie got behind him and bellowed in his ear: "I'm Vinnie Jones. I'm a fucking gypsy. It's just you and me today, fat boy ... " Gazza, despite all his cockiness, was shitting himself even before the assault happened.

Today, I can't honestly think of a comparable figure. Vinnie looked and acted the part, almost a pantomime baddy, but they don't build them like that any more. Modern footballers are more like ballet dancers, thin and slender. They're taller than they used to be, on average by three inches, and about a stone lighter. I did actually do some proper research once, when I was really, really bored, going through my programmes comparing Cup final teams from the 1930s with those from the 1990s. Today, Thierry Henry is how they'd all like to look—and play.

Robbie Savage gets booed by the opposition, and he does put it about, but he's in the Blackburn team for his enthusiasm and hard work. Kicking their best players up the arse, that's an optional extra. There must be some old-style thugs, in build and character, in the lower divisions, but I can't think of any in the Premiership. Claude Makelele is probably the best midfield stopper, but he's quite small, doesn't glare and scowl, and is certainly nowhere as vicious and vindictive as Roy Keane. Keano saw his job as intimidating his own players as well as the opposition. He could take it and not moan, but that commonly was the mark of the hard man: show no weakness.

One of Sven's problems is that we are no longer breeding midfield enforcers, trained to break up the opposition's players, or their legs. Steven Gerrard has been tried, but he's not a reliable tackler. Michael Carrick is being touted for that position, but he's a powder puff. One glare from Vinnie and he'd faint.

I wonder if it's anything to do with nomenclature. Until recently, young professionals started as "apprentices", and then graduated to "the stiffs". All very workmanlike. Now they graduate from "academies", as if they were intellectuals, eating pasta, supping red wine, wanting to be creative.

Yes, of course, Keane was good, excellent even. I'd always much rather have had him in my team than against. And all players, even the most creative, have a nasty streak. But Keano was a role model with a nasty role that football is now choosing to do without.

When I was 18, mum binned my scrapbook and let out my half of the bed

5 December 2005

MY FIRST CONSCIOUS MEMORY OF A BIG FOOTBALL game was Moscow Dynamo against Glasgow Rangers. They arrived in Britain exactly 60 years ago, in November 1945, to play four friendly games. They were the first Russian club to come here, and the first of our post-war foreign visitors. The whole country was fascinated. They seemed so exotic, as if they had come from outer space to lighten and brighten our dull, deprived, depressing post-war days.

I was nine at the time and living in Dumfries, and I read every word I could about them, cutting out their photos and match reports and sticking them in my scrapbook. I used a home-made paste of flour mixed with water. It made their faces and bodies horribly soggy, but overnight they would stiffen, and next morning they would be sticking up on the pages as if they had come back to life, turning almost three-dimensional.

Everyone was amazed and amused when, before their first game, against Chelsea, the Russians presented bouquets of flowers to the opposing players. They were so embarrassed, didn't know where to look. Real men—in fact, any men—in the post-war years would rather be seen dead than holding a bunch of flowers. Almost as shaming as pushing a pram or changing a nappy.

Over 85,000 at Stamford Bridge saw a 3–3 draw. They then played Cardiff City, whom they stuffed 10–1, but most of the Welsh team had come straight out of the pit before kick-off. Back in London, they played Arsenal at White Hart Lane; Highbury had been taken over for war purposes. Dynamo won 4–3 despite Arsenal fielding our two Stans, Matthews and Mortensen. There was such a thick fog that, in the second half, Dynamo supposedly played with 12 men, unseen by the ref. Their final game was at Ibrox against Rangers—the one I was most interested in, being Scottish. Over 90,000 saw a 2–2 draw.

The Russians brought some dodgy-looking security men and probably a few spies, using the tour for propaganda as well as football purposes. They also brought their own food, knowing we were still eating rubbish wartime rations. My mother used to give me mashed parsnip, swearing it was bananas, which I believed, never having tasted or seen a banana.

Oh, how I wish I still had that scrapbook. My mother threw it out when, at 18, I went off to Durham and she let out my half of the bed, which I shared with my brother, to a lodger.

About five years ago I managed to buy a Chelsea-Dynamo programme, but until a week ago I'd never come across or even seen copies in any books of the other three programmes. Then I suddenly spotted all four of them, Lot 149, in Graham Budd's latest football auction with

Sotheby's at Olympia. So I went along to bid. Some stuff was fetching huge amounts, such as a 19th-century mirror from a Glasgow pub, painted with a football scene. In the catalogue, the estimate was £6,000–£8,000. It went for £14,000. Strewth. Then an Arsenal programme for their first game ever at Highbury in 1913 made £5,600 as opposed to an expected £1,500.

It was estimated that my lot would go for £500–£600. Yes, I know, madness. My hand was sweating as I held my little paddle aloft, the one you use for bidding. But I got it. Won't say what I paid, in case my wife reads this.

Coming home on the bus, I could hardly contain my excitement. Along with the four programmes was a little scrapbook, done on a school exercise book by a Glasgow schoolboy, George Campbell. His school is not named, but in November 1945, he was in Class 4, Lower Science. His cuttings have been immaculately stuck in, using real glue, and he's written his own captions, in ink, to the cut-out newspaper photos, which cover all four games. Clearly a very neat and tidy boy. I wonder what happened to him. If you're still with us, George, well done and thanks. I'll treasure it for ever, as long as I'm here and following football.

Even girls who've never been to a match can spot a footballer three blocks away

12 December 2005

I WAS HAVING LUNCH WITH MELVYN BRAGG AT A restaurant in Hampstead village, the Villa Bianca. We go back a long way, me and Melv, more than 40 years, both coming from Cumbria around the same time, then having the same agent, same accountant. My wife and I were with him the night that Kennedy died, having dinner, which has turned out pretty handy, whenever people ask where were you when JFK was shot.

They say blokes don't retain their friends as they go through life, which is roughly true, compared with women, who keep up the girly stuff all their lives, with letters, regular phone calls, coffees and such. But I have six chaps from my life I have lunch with once a year to catch up on vital things, like last night's football, children, those bastards at VAT.

It was quite busy, mainly with women who lunch, and I could sense them giving little nudges, don't look now, I'm sure that's Melv, what lovely hair. Melvyn was taking no notice, as if unaware, but then he's used to it. This is not always the case with famous people. Some do play to the gallery. In my long-legged experience of being out and about with famous faces, I always thought Paul McCartney enjoyed it. Gazza doesn't mind it either, as long as he's not down, depressed. And he'll sign autographs for ages.

Into the restaurant came a little group of fairly scruffy young people in jeans. There were three in their twenties, one a woman with a baby in a pushchair, plus an older man who might have been the father of the woman. There was a little bit of waiter fussing, but not much, arranging the table, making enough room for the pushchair.

The newcomers had been given the table next to us, so I wasn't best pleased when I noticed that one of them was smoking. Should I call a waiter, object, say it could bring on my asthma? Then I realised they were all speaking French. Huh, frogs, what do you expect, they smoke everywhere. Then I recognised one of them.

"Don't look now," I said to Melvyn, who had his back to their table, "but Robert Pires has arrived ... " Melvyn did, of course, after only a very slight pause, pretending to turn to look at something else. "I think I'll go and tell him he played well last night," said Melvyn. We had both been at the Arsenal game the night before, and it was true—Pires had done well. Melvyn is a real Arsenal fan, unlike me, and he does speak good French.

One of the four, the youngest, had his back to me, so I couldn't quite see his face, but it struck me he looked very like Gael Clichy, Arsenal's young full-back, who is often in the first team. I would like, for academic reasons, to know how he himself pronounces his surname. Can it really be like "cliché", a French word we have pinched?

Melvyn's interest was interesting. One forgets that

famous people can be fans, just like the rest of us, unable to resist gaping. I exclude my wife from this wild generalisation. Her first instinct is to cross the road, should she spot a Face. But then she's not normal. I remember being struck by John Lennon telling me how thrilled he was to have got Little Richard's autograph.

Footballers today are probably our most famous famous people, more quickly recognised than royalty, pop stars, politicians. In the old days, they remained on the back pages, and only real diehard fans, who went to every home game, or collected cigarette cards, could spot them in mufti in the street. Now, top Premiership stars are on all pages and constantly on TV, in close-up for 90 minutes, so that every mannerism, every haircut, gets known to millions. Dopey girls in clubs, who have never been to a game, can spot them three blokes, I mean three blocks, away. Then they pounce.

In the end, Melvyn didn't talk to Pires, deciding to leave him in peace. Very wise. But I would like to have known how to pronounce Clichy.

2006 — World Cup: I was there in '66. Now, eagerly if warily, I'm plumping up the sofa for another great World Cup

19 December 2005

I'VE FILLED MY DIARY, INSERTED ALL THE ENGLAND games and every other one, put special marks on the kitchen calendar, told the wife and other domestic and family persons that that will be it, during those four weeks from 9 June to 9 July, I won't be accepting calls from human beings or taking part in any sort of family life, is that clear? Right, think on.

By an amazing bit of good luck the annual general meeting of the Cumbria Wildlife Trust, of which I am president, is on 8 June, the day before it all starts. During the past three World Cups there's been a clash with the AGM and I've had to miss one game, something absolutely vital like Ecuador *v* Croatia (1–0 in 2002, as I'm sure you remember). This time I've made sure that my diary, and my life, have been totally cleared. I'm so excited. Can't wait for the special pull-outs, World Cup souvenirs, posters, stickers, badges. I do hope Sainsbury's is doing World Cup medals with the phizogs of the England squad. I'll be collecting them, don't you worry, son.

I like the fact that, in World Cups, money can't buy success the way it can in league football. Clubs such as Chelsea or Real Madrid can open their cheque books and buy anyone, from anywhere, regardless of where they were born. The players might kiss the club badge when they score, but we know it's a nonsense. They're all mercenaries, ready to kiss any old badge if the money's good enough.

In the World Cup you get minnows who in theory have no right to be there. This time we'll have countries like Costa Rica (population four million) and Trinidad and Tobago (just over a million). They start out on level pegging with giants like Brazil (180 million) and the US (295 million). Every four years there are one or two titchy countries that by chance have been blessed with three or four half-decent native-born players and have somehow managed to get through all the qualifying hoops.

I'll be keeping a particular eye on Trinidad and Tobago, not just because they are the smallest country, but because their captain is Dwight Yorke. I did his biography six years ago, when he was winning the treble with Man Utd. He messed me around, was always late, not really interested, which really pissed me off and I've moaned about him ever since. But now I've found myself saying, oh yes, my friend Dwight, wonderful person, inspirational captain. You haven't got a spare ticket, have you, Dwighty?

I like to think World Cups encourage the sort of sportsmanship you don't normally see in league football. The players know they are on a world stage, all eyes on them, representing the honour of their country, so they tend to desist from cheating, conning, diving, fighting, trying to maim each other. Well, most of the time.

For about four World Cups I got my children to do little charts listing the populations of all 32 countries, then at the end we would work out the real winners, based on points won for every million of their populations. By this reckoning Trinidad and Tobago should be top this year, just as long as they can scramble one point. It was good practice for the children's sums, so I maintained, and their geography, but now they've left home, out in the world, they won't help me. So selfish. But I have hope for my two grandchildren, aged six. They're a bit young to do the maths, but I plan to get them a world map each and we can find all the countries. Awfully educational, World Cups.

And the history, that's jolly interesting as well. Fifa, the world body, was created in 1904, but England, along with Scotland, Ireland and Wales, refused to join. We invented football, so who do these foreign johnnies think they are, coming along trying to organise our game? "Fifa does not appeal to me," said Charles Sutcliffe, a member of our FA, in 1928. "I don't care a brass farthing about the improvement of the game in France, Belgium, Austria or Germany. An organisation where such football associations as those of Uruguay and Paraguay, Brazil and Egypt, Bohemia and Pan Russia, are co-equal with England, Scotland, Wales and Ireland seems to me to be a case of magnifying the midgets ..."

The first World Cup, held in Uruguay in 1930, went ahead with no British involvement. Only four European countries made the trip—Belgium, France, Romania and Yugoslavia—and they all went on the same ship, which took two weeks to reach Uruguay. The players exercised on the deck to keep fit. On board was Jules Rimet, the French lawyer who was president of Fifa, carrying the World Cup trophy in his luggage. Thirteen countries in all competed. Uruguay beat Argentina 4–2 in the final.

England finally joined Fifa after the Second World War, in time to take part in the 1950 World Cup in Brazil—and suffered the humiliation of being beaten 1–0 by the US in the first round. What a shock. That was when we realised the rest of the world had indeed progressed.

But of course it all came right in 1966—and I was there, at Wembley, for the final, in seat 37, row 9, entrance 36, K turnstile, price £5, one of the best seats. I got it through a friend, now dead, called James Bredin, who was boss of Border TV. He even took me there in his chauffeur-driven car. Bliss.

We have been rubbish since, sometimes not even getting to the finals. It might well have been due to that nasty old British habit of superiority. Because we won, we thought it proved we were the best again, that we had nothing to learn from foreigners and had no need to reform our training methods. Now, 40 years later, thanks to all the foreign managers and foreign players and the TV money, the standards of the top Premiership teams are as good as anywhere's.

Our national team doesn't have a British-born manager, which is a bit of an embarrassment, if we are now supposed to be so good. In fact there is not one Briton among the 32 managers. Holland, a much smaller country, has got four in charge—of South Korea, Australia, Trinidad and Tobago as well as Holland. But this time we have by chance managed to throw up half a dozen native-born players who can be considered world-class—Beckham, Lampard, Gerrard, Terry, Rooney, Owen—players who would probably make it into the squad of most countries. Apart from Brazil. Once again Brazil appear to be peaking at the right time. They have ten players, some of whom we'd never heard of till recently, who are all world-class. However, it does look as if we have our best chance since 1966. I think we will get to the final, but won't win. On the other hand, we could easily get stuffed by somewhere like Trinidad and Tobago.

The 31 other countries have used a total of 137 players who play in England. Chelsea, for example, have 17 foreign players who are likely to play in Germany, plus their seven English players. So, whichever countries are playing each other, it's more than likely we'll be able to cheer on some of "our lads", out there, on the pitch.

What had happened to Harry Kewell? Had a bird decided to nest on his head?

9 January 2006

ONLY HALF A SEASON TO GO TO THE WORLD CUP, SO time to read the runes, and the Rons, and the Roons—goodness, there are just so many Do Ron Rons in football these days.

Hair. After almost a year now of boring haircuts, Liverpool's Harry Kewell is playing a stormer. At first I wasn't sure if he knew what had happened to him. Had some strange bird decided to nest on his head? Did he overdo the energy drinks and were they turning him into a sumo wrestler? But no, after careful examination, I'm convinced it's deliberate—and totally brilliant. He acquired not just one but two ponytails, one above the other. Look out for one or both in the World Cup when he turns out for Australia.

Arse. Upon which Arsenal might fall. How awful it would be if, when they move into their amazing new stadium next season, Spurs have ended miles above them in the League, they are not in Europe and Thierry Henry has left. It'll be so sad, hee hee hee.

Foot. Wee Michael's, of course, for which a nation prays. I was at that game, against Spurs, when it got broken in the last minute of the first-half, yet nobody where I was sitting in the press box realised. Even when Owen didn't come out for the second-half, no one knew the reason. All the talk at half-time was about a Press Association reporter, three along from me, who headed a miskicked ball back into play.

Talc. How do you think it has a use in football? Apart from in the dressing room. I was watching a South American league game, late one evening, nothing else to do, when the ref awarded a free-kick just outside the box. Knowing the defending team would play silly buggers and not get back, and the attacking team would try to move the ball when he wasn't watching, he took some talcum powder from his pocket and marked the exact spot from whence the kick had to be taken. Wasn't that clever? And yet nothing to do with modern technology. Do hope it features in the WC.

Gloves. As worn by a referee—also something I'd never seen before. Dermot Gallagher wore a pair of leather ones over the Christmas period for a Second Division game. What a softie. But why didn't he wear a woolly hat to warm his baldy head?

Notice. The one I pondered longest was a huge one, the length of the grandstand, at a Motherwell-Aberdeen game: "Keep cigarettes away from the match." I thought at first it might be a security message, then realised the pun. All it was saying, I presume, was "don't smoke at the game".

Emotive phrases. I've written down quite a few this season when listening to commentaries. "Gerrard opened his body." That did present some horrific images. As did "Lampard has managed to get his leg over". But my favourite so far has been "Dunn stuck out an important leg". As opposed to his ordinary, trivial leg, the one he never uses.

Weird adverb. As used by Clive Tyldesley in his report on the Monaco-CSKA Moscow Euro game. "The pitch is infamously laid on a car park." Which it is, but what was the adverb he was struggling and failing to find? I spent the rest of the match obsessed with trying to help him. "Notoriously"? No, that would have been just as bad. "As is well known" would have been the best way out. Unless he knows something about the architect that we don't know.

Message. I longed to know why José Mourinho gave Carlton Cole, coming on as sub, a written message to pass on to John Terry during the Chelsea-Manchester United game. Both Cole and Terry are English — so why couldn't it have been a verbal message? Could he not trust Cole to remember it? It was a long way across the pitch. Do they not speak to each other? Or perhaps it was a drawing.

Or a joke. That must have been it, such as one I got in a Christmas cracker: "Why is a football ground so cool? Because it's full of fans."

Right, that's it for now. Off for my hols in the Caribbean. See yous next month. Please, please, o bon Dieu, let nothing happen to Roo Roo Rooney while I'm away.

Who would I pick for the job? Hiddink

13 February 2006

I ALWAYS DREAD DURING MY THREE WEEKS AWAY every January that something really awful terrible frightful will happen in my absence and I won't know about it until long after—something absolutely earth-shattering, like Rooney getting injured, Carlisle United collapsing, or Spurs signing another dozen midfield nobodies.

For the first two weeks, I was well in touch. At breakfast at Cobblers Cove in Barbados you get given a four-page faxed digest of the British news, plus that morning's *Barbados Advocate*. Cotton House in Mustique now does even better, giving you a copy of almost any morning paper you might want, from anywhere in the world—the whole paper, not a digest—taken from the internet but printed locally. It meant I was reading that morning's *Times* earlier than I can read it in London. Those are the perks you get if you stay at a posh hotel.

But in the third week, we were in a rented room in Bequia, a little island in the Grenadines, cut off from all news, with not even a local paper to read. It was agony. Sorry, just slipped out. Yes, of course, pet, we don't go to the Caribbean to worry about stupid football results and transfers. How could I have even thought of it?

The minute I got home, I found that something BIG had happened during that last week. And it wasn't something I dreaded, but excellent news: Sven has got the push. Naturally, it should have been kept quiet that he's going after the World Cup, just as Tony Blair should have kept private his intention to pack it in. It's unnecessarily unsettling for all those concerned when such things are known so far ahead.

So who'll get Sven's job? I see it as only a part-time occupation, suitable for someone of mature years, whose whole life revolves around watching football, and who never leaves before the end; who will not get into a leg-over situation in the office, mainly 'cos he would work from home and anyway his leg is too knackered. Yes, I'm thinking about myself. I could do it. No problem. Got my own pencil.

Alas, I fear the FA will not be so sensible, preferring someone younger with a proven track record in professional football. Someone, say, who earned 57 caps for England, starred in a World Cup semi-final, who has had experience of playing in Italy and China as well as top clubs in England and Scotland, who has already made his mark as a coach — in fact they still talk about him with some awe and wonderment at Boston United and Kettering. Yes, step forward Gazza.

Well, if Jurgen Klinsmann can manage Germany at a similar age, and with no coaching experience, and if Stuart Pearce, equally young, seen as a thicko and known as Psycho in his playing days, has now turned into a serious possibility, then the FA may well surprise us all with someone unexpected and inexperienced.

But I'm sure they'll play safe, go for someone with a good track record as an international manager, who knows the world scene, has managed in many countries, which none of the English-born contenders like Curbs, Big Sam and McClaren have done; who is mature, yet shows he still cares passionately about football and not just the money, unlike Sven; someone who has done an excellent job with unfancied countries like South Korea and Australia, and would now see managing England as a step up and an honour.

Yup, Guus Hiddink. He is the one I would pick. Who cares if he's foreign? The Dutch speak better English than most English players. True Brits like Kevin Keegan, Glenn Hoddle and Graham Taylor didn't do nuffink for us. So many of Britain's big firms and institutions are now run by foreigners. We're a multi-cultured country.

And who minds if, as a single man, he could be caught with his leg over? *The News of the World* has got to have its fun. Girls need kiss'n'tell money. And Scottish sub-editors will really enjoy playing with his name. Guus is apparently pronounced "hoose", as in "there's a wee moose in the hoose". Let him in, I say.

For football stars, writing a book is easy. It's promoting it that's the killer

20 February 2006

DID THE YOUNG MOZART GET A FIVE-BOOK DEAL FOR £5m when he was only 20? Course not. He was just a run-of-the-mill genius. Didn't even play away games till he was six. Or Shakespeare? No chance. He was still hanging around the back alleys on his council estate in Stratford-upon-Avon, though he had met and married Anne Hathaway by then—without getting a penny from *Hello!* for the wedding. Backward or what?

Wayne Rooney, he's the boy. HarperCollins is reported to be paying him £1m a shot for five books. He has had a long and amazing life. You couldn't get it all into just one book. But it will be hard work. From my own experience of celeb biographies, I would say for the first book he should allow three hours a day talking to his ghost writer, for six days, preferably spread over six months. That should do for the words, which he never need read.

The really knackering bit, Wayne, is to come. I dare say you haven't read the small print, but I reckon you'll have to spend twice as much time on personal appearances. Let's say five days of bookshop signings in London and the provinces; five days doing Richard and Judy, TV and radio stuff; then four days behind the scenes, glad-handing the trade. It will be written into the contract, the exact number of days, and this is what will sell the book. I'd rather be tackled by Robbie Savage.

If you sign till your right hand falls off, smile till your teeth ache, then your publisher should get its first million back in six months—£250,000 to £500,000 for the serial rights, plus the profits on 300,000 hardback copies sold.

I've just been to Headline's sales conference, held at an utterly swish hotel near Marlow where about 80 people stayed overnight in total luxury, then had a slap-up dinner. Limousines took the authors back and forth. Everything was on the house. We even got going-away presents. There were three famous football persons present, whose books Headline is publishing. (Plus moi, as I have my memoirs out in August, but this is not a plug, certainly not, just to explain why I was there.)

Rio Ferdinand arrived bang on time, despite having played for Man United the night before and been sent off. Gazza was there, having just flown in from a clinic in Arizona, and being about to go off to Dubai. It's in their contract, see. Tommy Docherty was the third famous name, but he appears to spend his time doing after-dinner stuff, so it probably wasn't such a fag for him.

As authors, what we had to do was charm the buggers, I mean buyers, from W H Smith, Tesco and co, the serial rights persons from the *Daily Mail* and *Sunday Times*—all the people who can make or break our books.

In the old days, say 40 years ago, when I had my first book out, sales conferences were chaotic, held in smoke-filled back rooms. Authors were shuffled in, given ten minutes to talk about their book, a sandwich, and then shoved out. Now it's so streamlined and classy, with cutting-edge videos giving the book info while you tuck in to a six-course banquet. Authors, especially celeb authors, don't have to talk or do any work any more. Just be there.

At this time of the year, thirty something lads and lasses from W H Smith, probably on piddling wages, get besieged by the whole of Bloomsbury, desperate for their presence.

On this occasion, the three football stars, at a little champagne party beforehand, did get up and say a few words—and each was excellent. They spoke fluently, without notes, made little jokes, were nice and humble, said how hard they would work promoting their book. Gazza said it was his third visit to the American clinic. He now gets a discount.

Tommy Docherty told how he was in a posh hotel once with Gazza when the waiter came up and said to Gazza: "Do you like scampi, sir?" Gazza replied: "I like all Walt Disney films." Gazza roared, genuinely, as the story was new to him. So Wayne, that's what you'll have to do. Smile for England.

I can get all the chat and analysis on footie that I need — in my head, son

27 February 2006

THEY ALL THINK, IN THE HOUSE, THAT I SPEND ALL my time either reading about football in the papers or watching it on television. If only. I must waste hours sleeping and eating, not to mention working. I really must try harder to put my life on this planet to better use.

As it is, there is just so much football I do not read about or watch, just as there is so much on the radio I always avoid. Not just Thought for the Day, as the whole nation goes to the lav when that starts, but anyone with a caring voice, such as Fergal Keane, that woman O'Leary, even Michael Buerk and John Humphrys when they put on their phoney, concerned voice to interview someone you've never heard of who has had to make some boring choice, yawn, yawn, or faced a supposed moral dilemma, God give us strength.

With football, I never watch the pre-match or half-time studio analysis. In the country, I have it timed to perfection. There are two fields I know I can walk around, leaving the house when the whistle blows and getting back exactly in time for the restart.

I never watch Saturday evening's Match of the Day

live—what, stay up till 10.30pm? It's not natural. I video it and then watch it on Sunday morning, whizzing on when it's a game I've already seen on Sky or there's any chat. I can get all the chat and analysis I need—in my head, son. These days, during the game itself, unlike being there in the flesh, you get immediate action replays of goals, saves or anything of interest or dispute. You don't need the "experts" to trudge through it all again later.

I reckon, when I have three live games in a day to watch, oh rapture, roll on the World Cup, that out of eight hours slumped in front of the telly, I can just nod off for two hours.

In the papers, I have loads of football topics that I never read. Last weekend, for example, before the big Liverpool-Man United game, when I saw acres in all the papers about Gary Neville slagging off Liverpool, I thought goody, I need never read a word.

Anything on diving, over which all the papers have been getting themselves into a self-righteous lather, I can skip at once. Ditto "will Wembley be ready in time". Supposed fights in the tunnel, disputed penalties, was it over the line or not, oh no, spare us. I miss everything that the TV time-servers call "talking points". They're all cobblers, rubbish stories, of interest only to desperate sub-editors.

Hooliganism: what are the Germans going to do about it, fantasy mobile brothels, eyes at once go glazed. World Cup ticket fiddles, as if I care. Managers getting bungs, dodgy agents, do us a favour, tell us something we don't know.

In *Four Four Two*, a magazine I love, which every fan

should read, the minute I see David Platt coming up, talking tactics with all his stupid diagrams, I run for cover. In *The Sunday Times*, whose sports section is excellent, I breathe a sigh of relief when I eventually get to Hugh McIlvanney, knowing he'll be pompously saying the obvious. With *The Times*'s The Game, which is the best daily coverage of footie, I never bother to plough through anything about money in football, or if they've got some dopey cause into their head.

When I'm jumping up in the middle of our family Sunday lunch to catch the live match, kicking off at the really stupid time of 1.30pm, I always tell them that if I were a true slave to football, I wouldn't even be sitting down at all. I'd have no time for eating, sleeping, breathing. In fact, you're lucky to see so much of me. Make the most of me when I return in 45 minutes, and don't scoff all the pudding.

I suppose, friends, it happens in all areas—art, literature, music. No matter how much we may love them, blind prejudice or total boredom in the face of certain artists, writers and composers, or when they get on to certain topics, means we should always manage some time for other things. Living, it's called.

There was outcry in Carlisle after the plastic sheep was kidnapped

6 March 2006

I'M SO 'CITED, AS ONE OF MY CHILDREN ALWAYS used to say. Going to see Real Madrid at Highbury, can't wait, compared with last Saturday when I woke up and thought to myself hmm, not much on today, Hunt, where are you taking me.

Neither Spurs nor Arsenal were at home, most unusual. What shall us do? Watch the rugby on telly? Nah. Watch the Scottish FA Cup? Hmm. I could go up west with my dear wife, if she'd let me, and have a culture blitz. Every Saturday she does an exhibition, then a theatre or film, but really, I've rarely trailed off to see anything cultural. Not since Glenn Hoddle retired.

Then I noticed that Carlisle United were playing at Barnet, just eight stops up the Northern Line. I rang my son, Jake. He hates me watching Arsenal, as well as Spurs, but approves of following Carlisle even from afar, as it's my home town. He said let's go, as long as you bring your stick. Cheeky sod.

Last season, Barnet were runaway winners of the Conference while CUFC managed to creep up through the play-offs. Early this season, Barnet beat Carlisle 3–1 at

Carlisle, a game I was at, and I thought heh up, we could be going down again. Since then, Carlisle have been near tops. Barnet have slumped.

On the Tube, we had the carriage to ourselves, oh if only getting to Arsenal and Spurs was like that, and I worried perhaps I'd got the wrong day, then it was a short pleasant walk to the ground. He who attends too many Premiership games can get tired of life. I'd forgotten that going to a game can be, well, so civilised. No obscene, heaving crowds, all bad-tempered or brutal. No nasty, smelly, lethal-looking burger vans.

Inside, it was quite noisy, all thanks to roughly a thousand CUFC fans who had made the long trek south, about doubling Barnet's normal crowd. (Their previous home game, against Lincoln, attracted only 1,695. The gate for Carlisle was 2,870.)

I talked to two CUFC fans, each carrying a sheep, not real, blow-ups, do be sensible. One told me how an officious steward at Shrewsbury had confiscated a blow-up sheep after it had somehow landed on the top of the Carlisle net. Carlisle's mass media, i.e., the *Cumberland News*, reported the story, which by then had become a kidnapped plastic sheep. There was a local outcry, naturally, then it mysteriously turned up for sale on eBay. It was bought for £60 and returned in triumph to Carlisle.

Carlisle have the biggest gates in League Two, home and away. Barnet's modest little, ramshackly Underhill Stadium made Brunton Park look like the San Siro. Two ends are overlooked by the backs of suburban houses. I stared hard—but no one was looking out from any window. I wrote down one of the stadium adverts: "Door too small, sofa too big? Call Translution..." You never know, could happen to me, though I hope never during a football match.

One of the Barnet directors told me they had their eye on a neighbouring site where they would like to move and build a new stadium, but some posh local residents were not pleased. Those who could be affected include... Arsène Wenger.

I also talked to Carlisle United's medical officer, John Haworth, and learned that for eight years he has been pushing for rugby-style "blood bins" in football. Teams with an injured player are often seriously handicapped when a player is off for some time being treated, while a doc doing stitches has coaches shouting at him, "Fucking hurry up, doc," which doesn't help the doc, the player, or the stitches. Far better for a temporary substitute to come on, thereby protecting players and docs. Doc Haworth now has the backing of the FA, the PFA and Carlisle's local MP, Eric Martlew, who has put down an early-day motion so far signed by 30 MPs. Good, eh? Things do happen at grass roots.

At Arsenal-Madrid on Wednesday the skills will doubtless be better, but I can't believe for one moment that I'll learn so many fascinating things. Carlisle won, by the way, 2–1. Cham-pee-ons.

Wainwright was cheering Blackburn on from the Fells last Sunday

13 March 2006

WE ALL HAVE TEAMS WE VAGUELY FOLLOW FROM A distance, often for pretty dopey reasons. I have a soft spot for Blackburn Rovers, though naturally I went along to watch them at Spurs last Sunday hoping they'd get stuffed. They have been creeping up the table recently, threatening Spurs's chance of Europe, which is a fat chance anyway.

As a boy, I liked the Rovers blue-and-white-chequered shirts, most distinctive. The comic papers used to print a page of football strips from every team in England and Scotland, which I would cut out and memorise. Ah, simple pleasures. I also like them because of Alfred Wainwright, whom I always thought of as a genius. No, he didn't play for them, or anyone else, though he sounds like a pre-war, no-nonsense centre-half.

A Wainwright, as he preferred to be known, was born in Blackburn in 1907 in a two-up, two-down terraced house surrounded by cotton mills. He left school at 13 and became an office boy at the town hall. After many years of night-school slog, he managed to qualify as an accountant. In 1941, he achieved his lifetime's ambition and moved to Lakeland, eventually becoming borough treasurer of Kendal.

His claim to greatness is his Pictorial Guides to the Lakeland Fells. Over 13 years, in his spare time, he climbed 214 Lakeland fells, getting to each on foot or by public transport, as he couldn't drive, then he wrote up his notes in little home-made books. They were miniature works of art, in that he drew everything by hand, the words and the illustrations.

In 1955, he began publishing them, originally at his own expense, exactly as he had written and drawn them, without an ounce of printer's type. By 1985, despite not a penny being spent on advertising, publicity or promotion, they had sold one million copies. Nor did he do any literary lunches, appearances or signing sessions. If he'd been starting today, no publisher would accept him. Wainwright loved the fells, loved animals more than humans, and always preferred to be on his own in Lakeland—and yet he also loved football, especially his beloved Rovers.

In 1939, while still living in Blackburn, he helped found Blackburn Rovers Supporters' Club, becoming treasurer, later secretary and chairman. In June 1940, he organised a coach trip from Blackburn to Wembley, where Rovers were to play West Ham in the war-time Cup final (Rovers got beaten 1–0).

After he had moved to Kendal, he still used to come down on the train to cheer Rovers on. Though not with his wife, Ruth, despite the fact that she also came from Blackburn, and enjoyed football. Their marriage, after only a few years, had become a sham, but as a local government official, he felt he had to keep up appearances.

It could be argued that his passion for the fells was partly an escape from a sad marriage. Perhaps football was another form of escape. A lot of us might identify with that, at least those who use it as a release from real life. Sometimes his wife, unbeknown to him, would catch the same train to Blackburn, making sure she was in a different compartment. She stood in another part of the ground, leaving before the end to get an early train back before he returned. Such pathos.

Wainwright died in 1991, by which time his eyesight had faded, but he still tuned in to Sports Report every Saturday at five to catch the results. He never lived, alas, to see Rovers win the Premiership in 1995.

But I'm sure he was watching the game last Sunday from somewhere above Haystacks. This is a fell near Buttermere where his ashes were scattered, at his own request. "Should you get a bit of grit in your boots as you are crossing Haystacks in the years to come," so he wrote in 1966, "please treat it with respect. It might be me."

And I bet he was well pissed off, as were Mark Hughes and the Rovers players. They dominated the second half and could easily have had a draw, but Spurs got the winner — in one fell swoop.

My view of Wayne has changed, but we still won't be going clubbing

20 March 2006

IF I POURED SCORN, FOUR WEEKS AGO, ON THE rumoured £5m being paid to Wayne Rooney, scoffing at the idea of a 20-year-old doing five books, suggesting he wasn't exactly Mozart or Shakespeare, then I was being patronising and silly as, of course, he is a young man of staggering genius and deserves 50 books, nay, a whole library.

Here's what's helped change my mind. I got this call from HarperCollins, from its head of sports books, a person I'd never met, asking if I'd like to come along to meet Wayne. I was, apparently, on a shortlist of three writers, all of whom were being invited into The Presence. My first thought was, huh, they don't know who I am; at my age and stature, I am long past taking part in a beauty parade, the very cheek. Then my second thought was, yeh, I'll be there.

Off I went last Wednesday afternoon. Waiting in the atrium at HarperCollins's mega-impressive Hammersmith HQ, I suddenly wondered if a certain distinguished sports journalist might be on the shortlist. I was jolly rude to him some weeks ago and heard he had vowed to duff me up.

I sat around for some time as Wayne was signing the

actual contract that afternoon, then doing a walkabout, meeting some HarperCollins staff. Eventually, I was called into the boardroom. There was Wayne's agent, Paul, an elegant woman I was told was his Brand Manager, another person in a suit introduced as his PR consultant, plus his own personal bodyguard. The presence of this last was reassuring, just in case anyone resorted to fisticuffs. Wayne himself was wearing a hoodie, trackie bottoms and trainers. He looked very young—tell us something new, Hunt—about two inches taller than I expected, calm, polite, relaxed, without any hint of arrogance.

I decided to ask him three questions. Why did he want to do the book? If he'd said for the money, or my agent thinks it's a good idea, I would have been worried. "So much has been written about me," he replied. "I just want to tell my own side of it now..."

Would he open up, reveal himself? When I did Dwight Yorke's biog, he was a nightmare—clever, fluent, but totally uptight, as opposed to Gazza. On my first meeting with Gazza, within an hour I was saying no, no, that's appalling, disgusting, I can't possibly use that in the book. Wayne nodded, appeared to understand and agreed he would co-operate.

I told him how much time I would need, how I would work, and asked about archives—had his mam or dad kept his local cuttings, his school reports, the first letters from Everton and other personal memorabilia? Yeh, they had, he said.

I managed to work in that I did not expect to be his buddy, going clubbing with him, but that he should look upon me as a Bobby Robson/Fergie figure. I'd presumed that at least one of the others on the shortlist would be much younger than me, so I wanted to pre-empt any ageist thoughts. I am, after all, old enough to be his grandad.

There is a well-known photo of Wayne on the beach on his hols, deep in concentration, as he reads the Gazza biog. In hardback. Big Spender. Paul, his agent, said they did think about sending in a bill for advertising.

I didn't mention my Wordsworth biog, as he might somehow have missed it. Not Willie Wordsworth, Carlisle's rugged and dour centre half in the 1930s, but William Wordsworth, poet laureate in the 1840s. I remember how, during it, I was effing and blinding, telling myself I'd never again write a life of someone who gets to 80. What a slog that was, so much to read and research. Took three years and I was knackered. On the other hand, writing the life of someone aged only 20 might pose certain, er, challenges.

On the bus home, I thought, well, if I don't get the gig, I have met him. Seems a nice lad. Two days later, the call came. I start next week. At the World Cup, I'll speak to him every day. Getting the gen. Can't wait.

Match-day hospitality is a nice little earner for yesterday's heroes

27 March 2006

PREMIERSHIP FOOTBALL BEGAN 15 YEARS AGO, bringing with it lots of excitements and improvements. Even the donkey in the first-team squad is now likely to become a millionaire. We have all-seater stadia, overpriced glossy programmes and games liable to kick off at really stupid times, but perhaps the Premiership's most distinctive feature is the growth in hospitality.

By hospitality I mean the corporate variety, covering private boxes, suites and dining rooms. It's also reached the lowest divisions, so that any local chancer, sorry plumber or solicitor, can entertain his clients with a nice seat, a free drink and a chance to vote for the donkey as man of the match, who, after the game, will appear at your seat, in person, and bray.

The big attraction, for clubs big and small, is that they can charge an enormous all-in price, about five times the basic seat. And the firms paying can justify the bill as promotion, or gorging, anything really, because no individual actually pays.

Oft have I cussed, at both Spurs and Arsenal, when hospitality guests fall late into their seats, their best suits covered in prawn sandwich stains, badges hanging from their red necks and no idea where they are or who's playing.

Until two weeks ago, I'd never actually been a hospitality guest, which explains why I'm such an expert. Then I got invited to Spurs. The hosping began four hours before kick-off with a pre-match tour, drinks and welcome pack, but I couldn't be fussed with all that, so I arrived just two hours before kick-off—in time for a four-course meal with wine and liqueurs.

I expected that by then it would be full of loud lads already the worse for wear, but it was terribly civilised. Around 200 were seated in an attractive dining room to enjoy an excellent meal. Martin Chivers, star of Spurs and England in the 1970s, was our host. During the meal he interviewed other stars on stage. A member of the Magic Circle came round the tables and did tricks. Warren Mitchell got up and told Jewish jokes, which is allowed, in fact is compulsory, at Spurs.

Two of the fans have realised the annual derby with Arsenal is being held on Yom Kippur. "What are we going to do?" wails one to the other. "I think we'll have to record it," replies the other. "What?" says his friend, "the whole service . . . ?"

What I wasn't aware of till later was that there were nine other such hospitality dining rooms, all of them with their own host, each a Spurs legend, such as Pat Jennings, Alan Mullery, Martin Peters, Phil Beal, Cliff Jones, John Pratt. I recall Pratt, a whole-hearted player, very helpful to me when I was writing *The Glory Game*, belting the ball over the North Stand into the Paxton Road. Never thought he'd become a Spurs legend. He is now. Altogether, at most home games, 3,500 people are enjoying some sort of hospitality at Spurs for prices ranging from £180 to £310 per person, depending on the package and the game.

I sat next to Martin Chivers, who has been doing this gig for more than 15 years. Weekdays, he's business development director of a property maintenance firm. Hosting hospitality is a nice little extra earner for players of his vintage. Until his sudden death, Peter Osgood worked as a match-day host at Chelsea. Charlie George does a similar thing at Arsenal.

Players from the Seventies, and even the Eighties, never made much money and never retired rich, so they are grateful for the work. But as Martin pointed out, the supply of celeb hosts available for football hospitality events will very soon dry up. First, many of today's stars are foreigners, who will retire to the place of their birth, planning never to walk down seedy old Tottenham High Road ever again. Second, whether Brit or foreigner, they will be too rich to be arsed with all this hospitality nonsense, glad-handing total strangers, telling the same stories and jokes for a measly few quid. It will be the end of an era as we now know it, and enjoy it. Which I did.

It's pointless saying this England squad's the best since 1966

3 April 2006

I'M A BIT WORRIED ABOUT ENGLAND, RATHER LIKE Mrs Dale used to say when she was worried about Dr Dale. They're beginning to look a bit peaky, off colour, picked up a touch of something, it could be catching—despite the fact that they haven't even started performing yet.

Like most fans, I veer between the most enormous hopes, buoyed up by little more than ... well, enormous hopes, and deep depressions centred somewhere over Northern Ireland which could well blow in and result in a horribly embarrassing defeat by Trinidad and Tobago.

On the one hand, I tell myself this is the best squad since 1966, hurrah for us. Look at all those world-class stars we have, isn't our Premiership the envy of the globe, so Sky TV tells us, wouldn't every team in the world like to have Wayne Rooney, so the back pages inform us? I go along with that most of the time, half thinking we are already in the final.

Then something happens to bring me back to cold reality, such as last week, talking to my dear friend Gazza. I was chuntering on, usual stuff, what a great squad, best chance for decades, blah blah, and he said to me, "What have they won?" The answer is: bugger all. Gazza at least did get to two semi-finals, of the World Cup in 1990 and the Euro nations in 1996, both times being beaten on penalties by Germany. According to José Mourinho, losing on penalties doesn't count, so you could argue that England did even better than the semis.

But this present lot, where are their medals? How far have they got in any World or Euro Cup? Exactly. Until they've done something, it's pointless to say they are the best since 1966. So I won't, not no more.

In fact, now that wee Owen looks well knackered, having another op, he might not even make it to Germany. Then who have we got as another world-class striker to play with Rooney? Jermain Defoe's disappeared down the pecking order. Crouch and Bent are scarcely Premier class, far less world-class, though I'd like to see both of them go to Germany, purely for their nomenclature. "Why did Peter Crouch?" so I ask my granddaughters. To which they reply, "Because he saw Darren Bent."

Then at full-back Ashley Cole is very good, but he's still injured, while on the other side we've got Gary Neville, who has improved these few years, but is still only adequate-to-safe and wouldn't get in any of the top ten national sides. Behind those two, rien, nada. Wayne Bridge and Andrew Johnson have been found wanting; Luke Young is second-rate. The trouble is that in the Premiership, almost all the decent full-backs are not English. G Neville should count himself lucky to be alive and kicking at this time.

I suppose Jamie Carragher could fill in and become a

world-class figure, if only for nose-blowing. Have you noticed how he does it with two fingers, grasping the top of his nose, and then emptying each nostril in turn? Awesome. I don't think the rest of the world will have seen such dexterity.

At centre-back, there's a good crop, with several to choose from. Few worries there. In the middle, we are also pretty well off, though the problem there is that Steven Gerrard and Frank Lampard tend to duplicate each other, so neither is allowed to play the dominating role each does for his club. And Sven doesn't help, with his lack of flexibility and feeble emotional energy.

We are jolly pleased with Paul Robinson as goalie, down here where I sit in the stalls, with the remote control, but close our eyes when David James lumbers on the stage. Goalies, though, tend not to get injured as often as outfield players.

So there we have it—two major problem areas, up front and at full-back, where the cover is pretty rubbishy. I'm going to keep reminding myself of this over the next ten weeks, whenever I feel irrational euphoria sweeping over me, or find myself being carried away with... nothing really.

The strength of a chain is in its weakest link. The strength of a team is in its weakest player. We could, alas, be carrying two weak links, come 9 June.

Hum, hum, hummin' along, I trace the songs that ring on the terraces

10 April 2006

WATCHING BIRMINGHAM CITY AGAINST CHELSEA last weekend on telly, I could hear from the first few minutes the strains of "Keep Right On To the End of the Road" being sung by the Birmingham faithful. I felt a sliver of pleasure. Not because I'm a City fan, or wanted Chelsea to get stuffed, which I did, but I was thinking, ah, isn't that nice—some traditions do linger on in this nasty, mercenary football world.

How long have City supporters sung that song? Dunno. But I know it dates back to 1918, and was written and sung by Sir Harry Lauder after his son was killed in the First World War.

Then there's "I'm Forever Blowing Bubbles", which is almost as old, 1919, but is American in origin and was performed in a musical called *The Passing Show*. West Ham fans took it over as their theme tune some time in the 1930s because, supposedly, one of their players had very curly hair and looked like the boy in the Millais painting Bubbles.

Even older in origin is the shout of "Come on you Irons" by West Ham fans, which must mean little to most non-West Ham fans today. It refers to Thames Ironworks, the club's original name when it was begun in 1895 by the owner of the Ironworks. In 1900, the club was reborn as West Ham United.

Charlton always step out on to their pitch to "When the Red, Red Robin Comes Bob Bob Bobbin' Along". I don't know its origins, but it sounds 1930s and American, and was probably adopted because Charlton play in red.

Everton's Z Cars theme tune, which accompanies them on to the pitch, is easier to explain if you are over 40. Otherwise, you have probably forgotten that excellent TV police series that was set on Merseyside.

Liverpool's anthem, "You'll Never Walk Alone", is a Rodgers and Hammerstein song from 1945 first made famous by Frank Sinatra. Gerry and the Pacemakers, the Liverpool group, got it to Number One in 1963, and then the Kop adopted it.

Spurs play "McNamara's Band" to greet the team, have done so for decades. I've always presumed it was a reference to Danny Blanchflower and his Irishness. I could be wrong.

The point of these songs, which fans on the terraces have passed on through the generations, is that every true-born Red/Blue/Lily White/Claret'n'Blue knows it is their song, which they will sing on the way to and from the game, in the pub, all the way to the end of their road.

Foreign players, however much they learn to kiss the badge, must have no idea of the significance of these fairly soppy, maudlin songs when they are being belted out so lustily by 30,000 swaying, waving fans.

They probably do actually recognise the badges, if by chance they have fetched up at one of our more famous clubs, and will also know the traditional colours. They will have grown up watching them on TV, reading boys' footie mags and the back pages in their countries' newspapers. But they're unlikely to know about the club's musical history.

Arsenal haven't got an old song that gets played or sung by their fans, but in the past they did have live music, performed by the police band that paraded up and down. Many clubs did something similar, usually with the local brass band. The leader would twirl his big baton and then throw it up in the air, and we all waited in anticipation for him to drop it. Arsenal's police band was the most impressive of them all. I have a match programme in front of me from 1954 which lists the items to be played, all of them light-opera or musical numbers. At the end of the announcement it states: "All engagements are by permission of the Commissioner of Police of the Metropolis, Sir John Nott-Bower, KCVO, and subject to the exigencies of the service." I treasure the programme for the beauty of the wording, not just the footer content.

Incidentally, it worked at Birmingham. They kept singing "Keep Right On To the End of the Road" till the last kick—and City got an excellent draw against a lumpen, boring Chelsea.

Arsenal may be foreign scum, but I still want them to win in Europe

17 April 2006

OH, I DO HOPE ARSENAL WIN THE EUROPEAN CHAMPIONS League. Been thinking it to myself for some time. Now I've said it out-loud. My son and all true Spurs fans will never speak to me again. Traitor, faithless, turncoat, blah, blah, blah.

True Arsenal haters believe you should never want Arsenal to win anything, ever. This year most of all. For if Arsenal win in the Euro, and Spurs finish the Premiership in fourth, then Spurs will not play in the Euro Champions League next season. That's the rules. Not that I understand them. Also, Arsenal are not just scum, but foreign scum.

Let's take the last first. Arsenal fans don't see foreign players, any more than they see black players. They see only good and bad players. Using a bit of dodgy spelling and verbal manipulation, Arsenal fans, as they cheer on their heroes, have persuaded themselves that, actually, their team is full of English players—viz Henry, Freddy, Bobby, Dennis, Robin, Percy, Alexander, Mathew, Gilbert, Philip. Viz, of course, he's foreign.

I want Arsenal to win because, since Christmas, they have been the most attractive team to watch in England—

closely followed by Man United. Some way behind come Spurs in third, with Chelsea, despite all their points, a poor fourth.

Obviously, as a Spurs fan, I want them to beat Arsenal when they play them next week, but apart from that game, I want to see Arsenal playing well, just as I want to see all teams playing well, expressing themselves, giving me something to enjoy and admire.

This hatred thing has got out of hand. We know that in Britain almost every club has a deadly rival, usually one which lives round the corner, yet the fans believe the competition are unspeakable creatures from outer space.

Dundee and Dundee United fans don't like each other—yet their grounds are only 0.22 miles apart. Then there's Notts Forest and Notts County (0.74 miles); Liverpool and Everton (0.79); Chelsea and Fulham (1.89); Villa and Birmingham City (3.5); Hearts and Hibs (3.5); Sheffield Wednesday and Sheffield United (3.8); Arsenal and Spurs (3.9); Rangers and Celtic (4.7); Bristol Rovers and Bristol City (4.8); Man United and Man City (5.17).

You can also hate clubs a bit further afield if they are seen to represent a rival city, such as Liverpool hating Man United and Cardiff City hating Swansea.

I didn't realise the depth of this latter hatred until I was watching the Football League Trophy Final (for clubs in the First and Second Divisions) at the Millennium Stadium a week ago. At the end of the game, which Swansea won, their star player, Lee Trundle, was seen holding a flag saying "Fuck off Cardiff" and wearing a T-shirt showing a man urinating on a Cardiff shirt. Yet they weren't playing

Cardiff—they were playing Carlisle United. Cardiff had fuck all, sorry, it's catching, to do with the event. It was just an opportunity on live TV for Swansea to rubbish their hated enemy.

I was cheering for Carlisle, my home-town team. Perhaps by growing up supporting them, I missed out on the hatred gene. Carlisle is so remote, so isolated, the players haven't got any neighbours, except sheep. And we know what they're good for. When I was a lad, there was a rivalry of sorts with Barrow and Workington, now long gone from the Football League, but it was pathetic. Nobody really cared, not in Carlisle anyway. We knew we were the superior Cumbrian team and city.

Today, I've noticed the local papers trying to work up an enmity against Darlington because, on the map, they appear to be the nearest rival in Division Two, but they're having a laugh. Historically, culturally, geographically, Darlington might as well be in Holland.

I never stand up, when they say stand up if you hate Arsenal. I don't hate. I love. Especially football. Right, that should get me into heaven, Premier Division.

Footie managers need a new signalling system. How about semaphore?

24 April 2006

I WAS IN THE PRESS BOX AT SPURS, ALWAYS SOMEthing of a treat, as they do a good steak pie at half-time, and you get a free programme, a free seat, lots of fascinating pre-match stats, a copy of the team sheet and access to the press conference of each manager afterwards. Could any fan ask for more?

On the other hand, its position is poor for watching the actual game. Up in the West Stand, above the directors' box, where I have sat for years, it's much better, giving you a plan view of everything.

I don't actually know why managers sit on the bench, when they can see so little. No wonder so many modern ones, such as Sam Allardyce, sit up in the stand, for the first- half anyway, communicating by phone to the bench. They like the immediacy, of course, the feeling of physical connection, the first-hand involvement with the players, which you do feel, at least with players on this side of the park. Those on the other side might as well be in Mongolia.

I always enjoy watching the managers screaming and shouting instructions and mostly, I suspect, failing to communicate. Players do nod back, even when they can't possibly have heard, clearly thinking, "Fucking hell, roll on the second-half when I'll be on the other side of the pitch and away from that bastard."

A lot of managers use whistling and hand signals, which presumably the players have learned to understand over the years. Perhaps they even practise them in training, after they've run through their goal celebrations and their diving in the penalty area. Alex Ferguson has a peculiar hands-raised-together movement, as if he's praying, which presumably means "stay tight". Pointing to your bonce is to tell them to concentrate.

Rafael Benitez of Liverpool does a sort of hand jive that's very complicated, but he almost does it to himself, as if he knows the players won't pay any bleedin' attention.

Anyway, watching the game at Spurs the other week, I wondered how things could be improved, because, at the moment, 80 per cent of what managers and coaches shout is being totally ignored. Written messages have been passed on to the pitch, as José Mourinho has recently done, but they're a bit slow. It also depends on a player being able to read, and in the right language.

Semaphore or some other visual symbols might be worth trying. I learned to signal in the Boy Scouts when I was 12, so surely modern players could manage it. If that's too complicated, a series of pictures could be held up, taken from the Janet and John books. Or the coaching staff could put on funny masks. Each image would indicate a new tactic. Anything to help save the manager's vocal cords.

Electronic boards might be better, like the ones the fourth official uses, and usually not very well, to tell us how many minutes of added time are to be played. Instructions would be signalled in code, so that the other team wouldn't understand. Or the big screen, which every big ground now has, could be used, as each club controls its own. Secret messages could be flashed to the home team only.

Ideally, each player would wear an earpiece, which the referees in rugby now have, so that every player could be controlled individually, like a robot. That would be every manager's dream. Even better, some sort of remote-controlled ECT equipment which would administer a nasty electro-convulsive shock to any player making a bad pass, missing a goal or, even worse, ignoring his stupid manager screaming from the touchline. That would larn them.

With the bottle-blonde wives and t-shirted uncles in the players' lounge

1 May 2006

IT WAS STRANGE, PUTTING ON A SUIT, COLLAR AND tie to go to a football match. Didn't seem suit-able. But my new best friend, Wayne Rooney, had said he'd leave me two tickets for Man United's game against Spurs at White Hart Lane, plus a ticket for the players' lounge. All these decades, friend of the stars, tra la, I'd never actually been in a players' lounge. That's why I thought I'd have to look vee smart. Players are very lookist.

The two tickets turned out to be with the Man U supporters in the South Upper Stand. I was taking my nephew Ross, who is a Watford fan, so he didn't mind, but I worried that I might jump up if Spurs scored and get my head bashed in.

I told Ross to listen to the accents, try to work out where the fans were from. All football fans believe that most Man United supporters come from Kent. Around us, we heard a lot of Welsh, some Italian, some Hindi, quite a bit of Korean—as both Park Ji-sung of Man United and Lee Young-pyo of Spurs were playing—but mostly they seemed to be from the London area.

And yet, when they sang the United songs, which they

did all the way through, they sang them with a Lancashire accent. Like parrots, they'd picked up the intonations with the words. I remember being in Russia and meeting some teenage Beatles fans who sang all the Beatles songs in a Liverpool accent.

When Danny Murphy, ex-Liverpool, now of Spurs, started warming up down below, they all shouted anti-Scouse obscenities and abuse. Then they went through several verses of a chant which ended with the line: "We all hate Leeds scum." I didn't hear one chant aimed at Yiddos, i.e., Spurs fans. I suppose there is no tradition of hatred between them.

There was a slight commotion in front of us when a bossy steward confiscated a large banner that some Man United fans had draped over the front wall. I asked him why, presuming the banner was either obscene or racist. It was neither. The reason was its size. It was so big that it had obscured the whole window of the £50,000 executive box below. I imagined them stuffing their faces with prawn sandwiches and warm Bulgarian wine when, wham, suddenly it had all gone horribly dark.

My new best friend scored two goals, so of course, the Man United fans went mad, singing his special song. I couldn't make out the words, nor could Ross, and he's got younger ears.

At half-time, I asked the man next to me to tell me the words to the Wayne Rooney chant. "No fucking idea," he said. "I've just come out of prison." Yet he had been standing up, mouthing the words as if he knew them.

I turned to a young man behind me and asked him.

"Dunno," he whispered. "I'm a Spurs fan." I asked what he was doing with the Man United supporters. "Friend of Rio's," he whispered.

I thought of asking the gaggle of Koreans to my right, but didn't think they'd know the words, and anyway, they were too busy posing for each other in front of their digital cameras. Then I saw a man and a boy of about ten who had both been singing lustily. He kindly told me the words:

I saw my friend, the other day
Who said he'd seen the white Pel-ay
Wayne Roo-nay, Wayne Roo-nay
He goes by the name of
Wayne Roo-nay.

I was looking forward to congratulating him afterwards in the players' lounge on his two goals, even though I'd have liked Spurs to win. But he never turned up. Nor did any of the other Man United players. I didn't even spot anyone from Spurs. It was full of Spurs wives, kids and families, more like a crèche than a bar, with a playpen and toys. The women looked anorexic and bottle-blonde, while most of the blokes, all forty something, presumably dads and uncles of Spurs players, had big bellies and tattoos on their arms, and were wearing T-shirts. I was the only wally in a suit.

Later in the week, when I saw Wayne again at his lovely home in Cheshire, he said: "Oh, didn't I tell you? We never go to the players' lounge. We're straight on the coach."

Talking to Wayne, early on Friday night, I asked how he felt about injuries

8 May 2006

THE WORLD HOLDS ITS BREATH, BUT IS THE WORLD getting carried away, English division? I don't suppose the Scots and Irish are fussed, but already in streets all over England there are cars flying English flags, some of them at half-mast, as we pray for Wayne's metatarsal to have a miracle recovery.

I did talk to Wayne on Friday night, before the Chelsea game, and asked him how he felt about injuries. Did he ever worry that one could ruin his World Cup, even his whole career? "I never think about injuries," he replied. "They don't enter my mind."

For the past three months I've been having a long weekly session with him at his lovely home in Cheshire, working on his autobiography—but for some reason, that was one corny question I had not asked him before.

Last week, we also talked about the World Cup. In Portugal in 2004, he was fairly unknown to the rest of Europe. Now he is aware that if he gets to Germany, he will be heavily marked, kicked and punched. "And behind the ref's back, they'll be stepping on my toes, trying to hurt ..."

From my point of view, nothing has changed, as yet. I

will be handing in the first 60,000 words next week, taking his life story up to this week. Then I have to hand in a further 10,000 words within 24 hours of England either getting stuffed or having triumphed, for publication at the end of July. Naturally, these words were going to be about the World Cup, with Wayne ringing me every day from the England camp. I was looking forward to that. But it looks as if he'll still be there, at some stage.

You could say that HarperCollins has got carried away, paying a reported £5m for five books about a kid who's only 20. On the other hand, George Best was responsible for about ten biographies, most of them repeating the same old stuff, and mostly done with hindsight. What HarperCollins has done, which is unique in publishing, is sign up someone ahead, before his career has hardly begun, like an investor trading in futures.

The plan is that a new book will come out every four years, coinciding with a World Cup. I don't know, just assume, that the publishers have built in escape clauses in case his career should come to a premature end. This particular accident is not in the slightest way career-threatening. It's the timing that is dramatic.

These past few months, I've been studying carefully the utterances of other England stars, such as John Terry, Steven Gerrard and Frank Lampard, and when asked the obvious question, "Have we got a chance?", they all name Rooney at once as the man who will give us that chance. This is unusual, for someone only 20 to have become a vital part of the team, and in such a short time. Sven did play him wide, early doors, but since moving to the middle, as second striker, he has become the focal point, as he has done for Man United. He can create, pass the ball and open up defences, as well as burst forward and score. He can be trusted to go back and defend without giving away silly free-kicks. This is most unusual, and why there is no exact replacement. And why oppositions fear him.

In football, one person can make a team — where teams are equal, with no glaring weaknesses. It then depends on a moment of surprise, from someone like Ronaldinho or Rooney, to turn the game around as Diego Maradona did for Argentina. They can have poor games, and other players, at World Cup level, can also do magic. But what has happened with Rooney is that in the team, he is the one they most look for, their talisman, their hope.

One could argue that Paul Robinson, the England goalie, is also irreplaceable, in that we all close our eyes when David James is in goal, but a goalie is there to save us from ourselves. Wayne is there to win it for us.

In the dressing room, he has also emerged as a character, a joker, which is not apparent in his public face. Gazza performed the same function and was equally loved in the England squad, but he was hyperactive. Wayne is calm, laid-back.

Sven will be taking a huge chance, should Wayne go to Germany not fully fit, but it will be worth it, to give him hope, speed his recovery, and cheer up the squad. And the nation. So, fingers and metatarsals crossed.

The Hunt Awards for Best-Dressed Man and Fairy of the Year go to...

15 May 2006

TEAM OF THE YEAR: CHELSEA DONE GOOD, BUT SO they should. Arsenal done gooder, but have won nothing. So far. Thus my team of the year is Carlisle United, for winning promotion two seasons running.

Fairy of the Year: Pascal Chimbonda of Wigan. Did you see him last Saturday in that final game, wearing gloves? Gloves! Almost 80°, well into May. Soft or what?

Best Dressed Awards: David Beckham is now a parody of a best-dressed player, so aware and so self-obsessed. Ditto José Mourinho, who has been wearing that boring black scarf, tied in that trendy way, even though our tortoise has long been out, which means it's summer, which means no more scarfs. José, get a grip. So, in first place is Mark Hughes of Blackburn. I have watched him all season on the touchline in his immaculate dark suit, sparkling white shirt, lovely tie, no creases. He does wear a traditional suit well. Every mother and grandmother must think, oooh.

In second place comes Mike Newell of Luton. Not seen much of him recently, but I do like his style, wearing a nice suit—but with what appears to be a white vest. Smart, yet ever so casual. And he never shows any emotion. That's so chic.

Sox of the Year: As worn by Thierry Henry. He pulls them up over his knees in moments of, well, I dunno. A secret signal? Let's hope Barca can't work it out.

Luckiest Manager: Steve McClaren. Not just for getting the job, but being so unpopular. Kevin Keegan and Glenn Hoddle arrived on a wave of national euphoria, and it did them no good. Better to raise no expectations. Has anyone checked the McClaren genealogy? Must be Scottish, somewhere, yet he got in on the English ticket.

Best Quote: "The game is very predictable, as we predicted." This was Bryan Hamilton, back during the African Cup of Nations finals. I wrote it down, and saved it. Can't waste a pearl.

Biggest Clichés: Everyone who has ever played for any team at any time for more than half an hour is now, wait for it—a legend. *The London Evening Standard*, writing the other week about Ian Wright, described him as "a one-time Arsenal legend". Surely a legend lasts for ever?

Mysteries of the Season: Well done to Reading, coming up into the Premiership, but what or who is their shirt sponsor—Kyocera? Is it a car, a tomato paste, a Korean porn film? In Europe, I would also like to know about Seville's shirt sponsor—Stevenson. Could they have the world's first literary shirt?

Farewell to: Alan Shearer, 260 goals in 427 Premiership games with Blackburn and Newcastle, and to Dennis Bergkamp, 87 goals in 253 appearances for Arsenal. Jolly well done—but please, please do not describe them as "loyal servants to football". Were they skivvies, on shit wages, with no rights, no freedom, sleeping in attics? I think not.

Suggestion for Next Season: Tape measures for refs. At present they pace out ten steps at free-kicks, but so many of them are huge lumps these days, such as Uriah Rennie and Steve Bennett, with very long strides, compared to Dermot Gallagher, who is small and weedy. And so the defence gains when it's a titchy ref. Come on, Wenger, why have you not protested?

Worries About Next Season: Now that Sultana, or whatever it's called, has got lots of TV rights, I expect fans will have to pay even more to get access to all the games. Players will demand more money, and get it. But what really pisses me off is the vast salaries that time-serving FA officials and talentless chief executives pay themselves for contributing nothing—purely for being jobsworths in an industry which happens to generate more billions every season.

Good luck to: Arsenal and Boro, each in a Euro cup final. Could England win both Euro pots, then go on to win the World Cup? Calm down, Hunt. Must be the heat, or these socks. I think I've pulled them up far too far. Can't breathe, let me out.

WORLD CUP, GERMANY 2006

Waiting for Wayne,
depressed by England,
the battle for
World Cup books

Settling in for the long haul —vino, crisps and pen to hand

12 June 2006

I'M EXHAUSTED ALREADY, AND WE'VE NOT YET kicked off. It isn't easy, pinning up all those World Cup wall charts, humping home 24 bottles of Beaujolais and 24 bags of crisps, "Less than half the fat of Morrisons standard crisps", so it reads on the bag. Who says I won't be eating sensibly this tournament.

During half-time in that warm-up game against Jamaica, when we were four up, I went out into the garden, sat down to have 15 minutes of sunbathing—and fell asleep. Well, it has been a warm week here in Lakeland. Good job my wife woke me and I got back to my action station, just in time.

I've told her the house rules for the next four weeks, as I do for every World Cup and Euro Nations. No talking. No entering my room during a game. Leave notes, if it's vital, but should you suspect I've fallen asleep, you have my permission to kick me.

It is going to be hard, as I plan to watch all 64 games, starting with three a day for the next two weeks. Good job I'm in training. All the years I've put in will now pay off. I keep notes on every match, dunno why, just habit, have done for the past four World Cups.

I haven't got any flags on my car yet. I don't think it suits a Jaguar, even one ten years old and bashed to hell. But every time I go into Cockermouth, they seem to be spreading like measles. Our vicar, who delivered our paper this morning, has once again got one on her car, and is wearing an England shirt. She is a sporty type, the Reverend Margaret Jenkinson. Was at the Olympics once, as a physio.

My wife has been into Carlisle, to a shop called Sports World, and bought the full England kit for the two-year-old son of a friend in the US. She won't tell me the price. I know it was expensive because it came with an inducement. She gets all her money back—if England win the World Cup. I've got the leaflet pinned up with all the charts and fantasy predictions.

This year, I've even more literature than usual, as I've subscribed to the England match programme. It's produced by Haymarket and gets delivered to your door on the day of each England home game. I'd somehow thought I'd get the World Cup programme as well. My mistake. It means the next one is not 'til 16 August against Greece. By which time the World Cup and Sven will be history.

It's full of glossy, whole-page ads for "England's Partners"—God, how I hate that term—such as McDonald's, Carlsberg and Pepsi. Ironic, really, that all three are products no modern footballer is supposed to use.

But having all the supplements, collecting all the stickers, flying stupid flags, being full of wild hopes and expectations, will count for nothing in the end. Fans know what to expect—utter agony.

The fun and enjoyment will immediately seep away as we hide behind the couch, waiting for Owen to get into the game, Lampard to wake up, Crouch to head the ball straight, Campbell to pass to someone on his own side, Sven to do something and not just sit there. And that will just be against Trinidad and Tobago. Heaven knows how we'll all cope when we're up against a half-decent team.

This World Cup, I'm also carrying the burden of Wayne's metatarsal. What a worry that's been, though I now feel confident that I could pass part one of my medical degree, with drawings.

The plan was to speak to him each day in Germany, then knock out 10,000 words for the final chapters of his autobiog. Will he play a part? Will England get to the final? And then, the biggest imponderable of all, will my wife get her money back on that England kit?

England's manager isn't working any magic on the team

19 June 2006

I WAS SO DEPRESSED AFTER ENGLAND'S FIRST GAME against Paraguay, I went into the fields and started lashing out, kicking the sheep, slamming gates, shouting at the thistles, looking for someone or something to blame. That stupid BBC studio panel, what idiots, telling us at half-time that England were doing great when they clearly were not. I screamed at them, but still they chuntered on, praising our lads.

Then I blamed German TV. What rubbish camera-work, shit reception. Imagine having that overhead screen, or whatever it was, casting giant shadows all over the Frankfurt pitch so you could hardly see what was going on. Didn't they know that would happen? It took me back to college hops in the Fifties, when they shone a light on a revolving glass ball during the last dance to make even the ugliest girls look moody and mysterious. At least when England gave the ball away, it made it harder to identify the culprit.

And I'm sure there was a hair in the gate. That's a technical term, used in TV, when something gets on to the camera lens. In this case it looked like fireflies, which were enlarged so much that it often seemed as if there was an extra ball whizzing about on the pitch. No wonder our poor petals were confused. Or it could have been my eyes. Or the Beaujolais.

Next day, I learned what the real problem was—the heat. I should have realised. Trust old Sven to point it out. He didn't know that at two o'clock on a June afternoon it might be hot. Not his fault. So I felt a bit more cheerful and able to appreciate some of the good things about the World Cup so far. The English language, that's a clear winner. The German announcers seem to use it first, before their own language. And during the opening ceremony, the first banner that got unfurled read "My Game is Fair Play". And there has been a lot of it, players helping up opponents they have just felled, giving smiles and handshakes.

The crowds have not been as colourful as in Japan and South Korea but the singing has been excellent: the German, Polish and Dutch fans chant away to exactly the same tunes we chant to, such as the ones which begin, "There's only one..." and "Stand up if you hate..." It would be helpful if one of the more educated commentators, for example Peter Drury, could tell us the words.

I take that back. He's so smug, self-satisfied, portentous, though not quite as annoying as Jonathan Pearce. "I seem to remember when, aged nine, the Mexican goalie opened a fridge and electrocuted himself... I seem to remember that the Iran winger once had a trial for Wolves..." Jonathan, we all know you've got it written down in front of you.

For this World Cup, Drury appears to be in tandem with David Pleat, who is boring rather than annoying. Pleat has got it into his head that the first words of his commentary must always be a greeting to us, the grateful viewers, who, of course, have been sitting panting for him to appear. "Evening all," he says, as if he's auditioning for Dixon of Dock Green.

I do know the real reason why I'm depressed and who is to blame—myself. Once I saw Argentina play, I came to my senses. How could I have got carried away? All the England flags, all the excitement, all the coverage, the luck of being in such an easy group, the number of highly talented individuals we happen to have, had led me, for a moment, to forget that Sven is a lousy manager. All this time, all this talent, and he still hasn't formed a team or a pattern.

Young Rooney has been fairly good at ringing me

26 June 2006

WHEN WAYNE RINGS ME FROM THE ENGLAND COACH after the game, or from his hotel room in Baden-Baden, I have this image of all the players sitting like school kids doing their homework. They speak with one hand over their mouths so no one can overhear. When writing, they have one arm over the page, so no one can copy. If they get desperate and can't think of what to say, they'll ask the person in the next seat or desk: "Come on, I helped you, I'm stuck, how much have you done, creep." "Oh no, not fair, that's cheating."

I did give Wayne, on his departure to Germany, an ever-so-artistic little notebook, pretty cover, not cheap, and a list of about 20 topics and questions to address each day, plus instructions to collect any leaflets for his scrapbook. I did this for many years with my own children when they went off on school camps. Wayne did smile, when I handed it over, and said he would try to fill it in.

I am pretty confident that he has not written a bleedin' word, nor even opened the notebook, but he has been fairly good at ringing me. The trouble is, because he has been The Story for so many weeks, a lot of the stuff he tells me for his book has been getting into the papers a few days later. And probably into other people's books.

There are at least five players working on their autobiographies at this World Cup. Rio Ferdinand and Ashley Cole are doing books for Headline; Frank Lampard and Wayne for HarperCollins; Stevie Gerrard for Bantam. There may be others I don't know about.

Unlike World Cups of the past, there has been a noticeable absence of first-person diaries by any of England's players in the newspapers. Every national paper used to have one, even when they were rubbish. I'd imagined it was because the players didn't need the money any more. They are so well paid, plus doing an official autobiography can make them a million, so why bother speaking to some sweaty tabloid sub.

It turns out that Sven has put his little foot down. He sent each player a letter saying that he did not want them writing or contributing to any first-person articles during the World Cup. (The only person who appears to have technically transgressed is Michael Owen—not in a paper, but by allowing his name to be used on a blog.)

Come the end of the World Cup, there will be a rush, not just for the best book, but to publish quickly. At the moment, touch wood, pencils sharpened, Wayne Rooney's book will be out first—just two and a half weeks after the end of the World Cup, which is when the last chapter will be written. This is incredible, in publishing terms, for a hardback book. Let me see, using all fingers, plus metatarsals, I have done 40 books in my long-legged career and on average it has taken a publisher nine months to get a book out. That's because of all the editing, legal checks, pictures, fitting in with PR, marketing and sales schedules, plus general faffing around.

My next book, for example—not the Wayne book, but my own autobiography, out in August, hurry, hurry—will have taken a year from writing the last word to appearing in print. Just shows what publishers can do when there's a lot of money at stake. I often wonder what ordinary publishing editors think of all this. They are ever so well educated and hard-working, but badly paid, yet they are sloshing around millions on footballers and other celebs who are already rich, knocking themselves out to make things work, and on time. It's the modern world, innit.

He's so tight-lipped that he makes the players nervous

3 July 2006

IN SOME WAYS, I WISH IT WAS ALL OVER. I'M knackered with the tension. Then I look on the bright side. Perhaps the secret of England's success in this World Cup will be playing rubbish all the way through to the final, plus the luck of the draw, plus better sides killing each other off. So we don't need England to get better, but stagger on, till they stagger over the finishing line. Four rubbish games down. Just another three rubbish games to go. Sorted.

At least the worst of the physical tension is over. I set myself the task of watching every live game, from two in the afternoon till ten at night, or 10.30 with extra time. So far, I have seen 48 games. Once the quarter-finals are over, with or without England, there will be a bit more space for, well, living.

Are you looking for sympathy? Did anyone ask you to do it? Do I have to ask you again: clear those empty bottles, crisp packets and dead fruit, bin those newspapers, pick up those cushions and, ugh, the smell in here — why can't you open a window? For 19 days, it's been like going on a long-haul flight every day. And as with long-haul flying, you tend to eat too much, drink too much, go into a slump, semi-dozing, semi-living, so you don't know where you are, which day, which country.

Good job I always fly club class. Here in Lakeland, I have my own cabin, a little TV room at the back of the house where I sprawl out on a couch and surround myself with goodies. The stewardess gets a bit ratty at times, but then they often do, bringing meals when you're not quite ready, wanting you to look at safety instructions when you're trying to work out what the referee Graham Poll is doing. Poor lad. For two seasons he's had Premiership crowds chanting, "Oh, Graham Poll, you're a fucking arse-hole", while managing to retain his superior smile. And yet, until that balls-up of a game between Oz and Croatia, when he gave out three yellows to the same player, and then that ref losing control in the Holland-Portugal game, I'd been thinking the World Cup refs had been doing pretty well. Most are so handsome, lean and fit, and I do love their ducky new outfits with the flash bit at the front. In fact, I'd just thought, with the proliferation of repro football shirts, why do you never see anyone wearing a ref's shirt? This World Cup could have started a new fashion, until Graham Poll came along.

So what is the point of the dinky little mouth mikes which look as if a white tapeworm has crawled out of their chops? Aren't they meant to allow a linesman or fourth official to tell the ref he's made a mistake? The other question is why England so often play badly in the second half, whereas, in the Premiership, our lads keep going to the end.

The answer is obvious—Sven. He's the difference. They come in at half-time, see him slumped or, at best, tight-lipped, offering nothing. On the bench he's silent, not like Scolari or most decent managers. Players might hate managers screaming and shouting at them, but it scares the shit out of them. When Sven does get round to changes, they are so often negative, making them more nervous.

One interesting thing about this World Cup has been the Germans no longer hating Jürgen Klinsmann for being an absentee manager. Living in California, he hardly saw any league games. Unlike Sven. He's trailed round hundreds—but he appears to have learned nothing. Watch him on the bench, dazed and stunned. It's as if he's been on a long-haul flight for the past five years.

Forget this World Cup nightmare—there's always Euro 2008

10 July 2006

SO WHO WAS TO BLAME? FIRST, SVEN. NO QUESTION. He had five and a half years, a very good squad, wasn't messed around, yet he was a lousy, indecisive, feckless, weak manager.

Yet, how we marvelled in September 2001 at the amazing 5–1 win over Germany. We could not believe our eyes as our lads played like angels and goal after goal went in. Now, I think it must have been luck. I can't remember one other game that made my heart soar.

There were moments during this World Cup: Joe Cole's goal-scoring volley from miles out against Sweden. What else? Becks's free kick? Jammy and long overdue. Those 60 minutes against Portugal when, down to ten men, they fought valiantly, but that's a negative image.

On paper, Sven could boast the best record of any England manager. Until Portugal, his success rate in matches played was 61.2 per cent compared with Alf Ramsey's 61.1 per cent. Now they are about equal—but, of course, they are not. Stats, as usual, lie through their teeth. Sven won lots of rubbish games—and not one when it mattered. Good riddance.

Second, the players. I blame them more than Sven. They couldn't help being badly directed. I'm sure in their own minds they tried hard enough. But they didn't play as well as they should have done. Their monster salaries don't get paid for fun. These are players at the top of their profession. OK, so none might be the current World or European Player of the Year, though Steven Gerrard made the shortlist, but at least five are rated world-class.

They also had great experience, were hardened by European and world tournaments, contained excellent captain figures such as Terry, Gerrard, Neville and Becks himself. Why didn't they lead and motivate? Why couldn't they pass straight or kick straight?

Maniche couldn't even make the Chelsea team, a pale figure compared with Lampard, yet there he was, a Portuguese star. Trinidad and Tobago, full of lower-division players, performed miles above themselves. France were supposed to be deadbeats, past it. Why couldn't the England squad raise or even play their ordinary game? It's a mystery.

Worst of all, they were nervous, tentative, lumpen, showing no swagger or pride. The lack of inner belief can be blamed on Sven but in the end, it was up to them. They bottled it.

I think next time we should ban them from press conferences. They all tried to spin it like politicians, telling us how the best was to come, rather than admitting any mistakes. Deep down, they must have known they were conning us.

Third, the one most of all to blame was me. Me, you, the

fans. We conned ourselves. How could we keep believing things would get better when the evidence was before our eyes? How could we have the best squad for 40 years when patently they had done bugger all to prove it?

We were amused by the behaviour of the WAGs, by the glitter and display of Becks's pre-World Cup Beckingham Palace swanky party, when we should have said how tawdry, such displays should be kept for when there is something to celebrate.

So, if we are disappointed and deflated, as I certainly am, we have only ourselves to blame. We led ourselves astray. But we'll do exactly the same again, in Euro 2008. Oh, come on. Wayne will be two years older, and wiser. Lampard and Gerrard will have learned to play together. Theo Walcott will be out of nappies. Inger-land.

What was all that about? The hopes and hairstyles at the World Cup

17 July 2006

THE FIRST THING I DID, ONCE IT WAS ALL OVER, WAS rush to Sainsbury's in Cockermouth where I knew, just knew, there would be some excellent bargains. And so it was that I bought ten England inflatable hands, in pre-tested sturdy vinyl, reduced to only 5p each. Could be my Christmas presents sorted. My second thought was—what was that all about? The World Cup, I mean?

Blond Ukrainians: Their team was full of them, yet I've been to Ukraine and never saw one. Mexicans without moustaches: another racial stereotype ruined.

Stereos still typeable: On the whole, the Latins *did* swagger, were more confident, skilful, while the north Europeans were lumpen, like England and Sweden, or, at their best, efficient like Germany.

Daft haircuts: Even Becks let us down, as he did in so many other ways. So the award has to go to Loco of Angola for his funny little quiff at the front. It made him look as if he was playing with sunspecs on his bonce.

Saucy commentary: "Lovely to see two strikers playing with each other." David Pleat on Germany during their semi with Italy.

Best team: I watched 57 games live and gave each team stars out of five for good play, skill, adventure. No one got a five-star performance. Germany got four stars three times, as did Argentina, followed by Italy two, France two, Brazil two, Mexico and Ghana one each.

Deserved winner: Italy performed well when it mattered, but in that final, there was little in it. If only England had performed well just once, they could have had a chance. Overall, looking back in my mind's eye, the Argies pleased me most.

National anthems: I loved them, especially seeing the Mexicans, arms across the tops of their chests.

Free-kicks: They were rubbish, on the whole, compared with Brazil of yesteryear. Corners, they were poor as well. And I don't remember any long throw-ins.

No new skills, movements or tricks: Except when Ronaldo of Portugal, in the match against Germany, treated us to a double back-heel click—which went straight to a German.

No appalling mistakes: No goalie made a total howler. The worst human blemish, alas, was Zidane's head-butt and red card.

The experts got it wrong: No one predicted an Italy–France final. The four main footer pundits on the *Sunday Times* each made Brazil the winner—and none had France even in the semi-finals. The bookies also got it wrong, ditto Fifa, which in its rankings had France at eight and Italy at 13.

Players predicted to do great but didn't Shevchenko, Ronaldinho, plus the whole of the England team.

Players rubbished for being oldies and past it: Zidane.

No ads on the shirts: Wasn't that refreshing. Now we'll be back to normal next season. Hide your eyes from the commercial glares.

Next season: We hope Sky TV will desist from praising our lads to the sky, 'best for generations', 'tra-la-la', 'full of world-beaters'.

New descriptions for next season: The Premier League—'best in England'; England team—'best in England' no let's say north of England, hold on, best in Cumbria, 'cos they have only one League club; Paul Robinson—'best goalie in Spurs team'.

So why did you buy those stupid inflatable hands? I like to think it's a confirmation of hope and expectation, that despite everything life will go on, there'll always be an England and they could be handy when doing the washing-up. Right, see yous next season.

POMONA BOOKS

POMONA IS A WHOLLY INDEPENDENT PUBLISHER DEDICATED to bringing before the public the work of prodigiously talented writers. Tell your friends. Our books can be purchased on-line at:

www.pomonauk.com

A free Pomona Sounds CD will be sent with every order.

ALSO AVAILABLE:

FOOTNOTE* by Boff Whalley

ISBN 1-904590-00-4 · £8.99

FOOTNOTE IS CLEVER, FUNNY AND IRREVERENT — A STORY ABOUT A boy from the redbrick clichés of smalltown England reconciling Mormonism and punk rock, industrial courtesy and political insurrection.

He finds a guitar, anarchism and art terrorism and, after years (and years and years) of earnest, determined, honest-to-goodness slogging, his pop group† makes it big; that's BIG with a megaphone actually. They write a song that has the whole world singing and, funnily enough, it's an admirable summary of a life well lived — about getting knocked down and getting back up again.

Meanwhile, there's a whole world still happening: authentic lives carefully drawn, emotional but not sentimental and always with a writer's eye for detail. *Footnote* is not another plodding rock memoir but a compassionate, critical and sometimes cynical account of a life steeped in pop culture, lower division football and putting the world to rights.

---

* See page 293 of Boff Whalley's book.

† Boff Whalley is a member of Chumbawamba.

RULE OF NIGHT by Trevor Hoyle

ISBN 1-904590-01-2 · £8.99

IF THE SIXTIES WERE SWINGING, THE SEVENTIES WERE THE HANG-over — darker, nastier, uglier — especially if you lived on a council estate in the north of England.

Rule of Night was first published in 1975 and has since become a cult classic. It pre-dates the current vogue for 'hard men' and 'football hoolie' books by 25 years.

It is, however, much more than this. Trevor Hoyle creates a chillingly detailed world, where teenagers prowl rainy fluorescent-lit streets dressed as their *Clockwork Orange* anti-heroes. The backdrop is provided by Ford Cortinas, Players No.6, the factory, the relentless struggle to maintain hope.

Hoyle, who has since been published by John Calder (home to Samuel Beckett and William S. Burroughs), has added a fascinating afterword to his original book which has been out of print and highly sought-after for many years.

• • •

THE FAN by Hunter Davies

ISBN 1-904590-02-0 · £9.99

HUNTER DAVIES IS ONE OF BRITAIN'S MOST ACCLAIMED WRITERS and journalists. He has written over 30 books, among them modern classics, *The Beatles* and *A Walk Around The Lakes*. *The Glory Game*, published in 1972, is a benchmark work on football and is still in print today.

The Fan is a collection of very personal, unusual pieces about his life as a supporter. He observes football in its sovereignty of the late 1900s and early 2000s and tackles the big topics of the day: Beckham's haircuts, high finance, the price of pies, the size of match day programmes, the enormous wages, the influence of Sky TV, England's numerous managers.

Along the way, he also lets us into his home life, in London and the Lake District, his family, his work, his tortoise, his poorly knee (caused by too much Sunday football).

Originally published in the *New Statesman* magazine, *The Fan* catches Davies at his very best and most amusing. It will appeal to supporters of any age, sex and loyalties.

LOVE SONGS by Crass

ISBN 1-904590-03-9 · £9.99

Our love of life is total,
everything we do is an expression of that.
Everything that we write is a love song.
– Penny Rimbaud, *Yes, Sir, I Will*

CRASS: A RURAL COLLECTIVE BASED IN ESSEX, FORMED IN 1977 OF A diverse and eclectic group of individuals who operated for several years using music, art, literature and film as vehicles to share information and ideas. They also wanted to change the world.

This is a collection of words spanning those seven short years; a book of shock slogans and mindless token tantrums. An anthology of passionate love songs that sought to inspire a generation, and succeeded.

• • •

SUM TOTAL by Ray Gosling

ISBN 1-904590-05-5 · £9.99

SUM TOTAL IS A LOST MASTERPIECE OF BRITISH LITERATURE, a restless, hungry riposte to America's finest Beat writers.

Written in 1961 when he was just 21, Gosling's itchy 'sort of' autobiography is a startlingly original take on the England of the early Sixties: rock 'n' roll, trains, dead-end jobs, drizzle, hitchhiking, jukebox cafés, trudging through hometown streets.

All the time he remains gloriously indulgent, disillusioned yet hopeful, tired but desperate for every new day.

Although now famous for hundreds of television and radio documentaries, in *Sum Total* Gosling reveals himself as a writer years ahead of his time, presenting a skew-whiff, arch and droll view of the world, both inside and out.

He has added a typically idiosyncratic and lengthy preface to the original text.

DIARY OF A HYPERDREAMER
by Bill Nelson

ISBN 1-904590-06-3 · £9.99

BILL NELSON IS ONE OF BRITAIN'S MOST RESPECTED CREATIVE forces. He came to prominence in the Seventies with Be Bop Deluxe and later Red Noise. He has collaborated with like-minds such as Yellow Magic Orchestra, David Sylvian, Harold Budd and Roger Eno and still releases a prolific amount of new music.

Diary of a Hyperdreamer is his day-by-day journal in which he ponders on life, art and the nation. His unique perspective is fed by a career creating and producing music, photography, painting and video.

Written from his home in a hamlet in north Yorkshire, he also includes engaging details of his family life, regular musings on mortality, along with reflections on his childhood and former life as a globe-trotting 'pop star.'

• • •

THE PRICE OF COAL by Barry Hines

ISBN 1-904590-08-X · £9.99

BARRY HINES IS A MASTER CRAFTSMAN. WHILE HE IS RIGHTLY celebrated for his classic, *A Kestrel for a Knave* (later filmed as *Kes*), his other work is equally powerful.

The Price of Coal is an uncompromising depiction of life at a colliery where beer, snooker, cricket and time spent on the allotment is the only respite from clawing coal from the earth.

A royal visit prompts the introduction of soft soap to the toilets, grass seeds scattered on the slag heap, and lashings of white paint across the site.

But when disaster strikes the superficial is forgotten as men fight for their lives in the darkness underneath collapsing seams of coal.

As ever, Hines proves himself an exemplary storyteller with a discerning eye for detail and when bolder, gaudier writing is long forgotten, his stays in the mind and nourishes it.

He has written a new foreword to the original text which was first published in 1979 and later adapted for television as two linked plays, directed by Ken Loach in the acclaimed *Play for Today* series.

LOOKS & SMILES by Barry Hines

ISBN 1-904590-09-8 · £9.99

LOOKS AND SMILES IS A LOST BULLETIN FROM THE EARLY-EIIGHTIES when the sun felt to have set permanently on hope and optimism. Unemployment was rampant, especially in the north where traditional industries were laid waste by Margaret Thatcher and her government.

Set amid this gloom, *Looks and Smiles* is an under-stated love affair between unemployed school-leaver Mick and Karen who works in a town centre shoe shop. They both want little more from life than a decent chance.

As ever, Hines proves himself an exemplary storyteller with a discerning eye for detail. He never resorts to sentimentality, and hope, however slender, flickers always.

The book was originally published in 1981 and later made into a film by Ken Loach.

· · ·

KICKED INTO TOUCH (PLUS EXTRA-TIME) by Fred Eyre

ISBN 1-904590-12-8 · £9.99

FRED EYRE'S SPORTING LIFE BEGAN FULL OF PROMISE WHEN he became Manchester City's first ever apprentice. He never made their first team. In fact, he seldom made anyone's first team. Injuries played a part but limited talent was the greater curse. As he plummeted down the leagues he had something few footballers possess: a stud-sharp memory and an ability to write humorously about the sport he loves.

Originally published in 1981, *Kicked Into Touch* has become an enigma — selling more than a million copies yet still retaining cult status within the sport and among fans. This new version has been completely revised, extended and updated with a new set of photographs included.

It is set to reach a new generation of football fans looking for an antidote to the glib reportage of a sport lost to show business.

MEAN WITH MONEY by Hunter Davies

ISBN 1-904590-13-6 · £9.99

AT LAST, A BOOK ABOUT MONEY THAT TELLS IT STRAIGHT: PUT IT under the bed. All of it. Sure, it makes for easy access to burglars but better them than the felons passing themselves off as financial advisors or acting as foot-soldiers for organisations with words like union, mutual, trust, alliance, equitable or assurance in their name.

Mean With Money, inspired by Hunter Davies' well-loved column in *The Sunday Times*, is wilfully short on practical advice but offers instead good humour and much-needed empathy as we face the corporate horror of high-handed and indifferent financial institutions.

Davies, one of Britain's most celebrated writers, also looks at ingenious ways to save money (cut your own hair, for starters) and what to do with it when it arrives. Along the way, he reveals details of his regular visits to McDonald's (it's free to use their toilets), the eccentric old ladies who staff his local Oxfam shop and the swim that cost him £333.

Famous for seminal works on The Beatles, football, and subjects as diverse as lottery winners and walking disused railway tracks, Davies is, once more, on top form. Go get 'em Hunt.

• • •

ZONE OF THE INTERIOR by Clancy Sigal

ISBN 1-904590-10-1 · £9.99

'THE BOOK THEY DARED NOT PRINT', ZONE OF THE INTERIOR IS a lost classic of zonked-out, high-as-a-kite Sixties literature. It tells the story of Sid Bell, an American political fugitive in London, who falls under the spell of Dr. Willie Last (partly modelled on the radical 'anti-psychiatrist' RD Laing). This unlikely duo feast on LSD, mescaline, psilocybin and psycho-babble, believing that only by self-injecting themselves with schizophrenia will they become true existentialist guerrillas. Their 'purple haze' odyssey takes them into the eye of the hurricane—mental hospitals, secure units for the violent, the Harley Street cabal of the 'Sacred 7' and semi-derelict churches that come complete with an underground tank for the woman convinced she's a fish. Sigal's approach is richly sardonic and anti-establishment, of both right and left, in a jazz-influenced free-form prose, comic and serious, myth-puncturing and elegiac. Along the way Sigal, now an established Hollywood screen-writer, makes the case for a revolutionary period of mental health nursing whose task is as yet undone.

THE ARMS OF THE INFINITE

by Christopher Barker

ISBN 1-904590-04-7 · £9.99

CHRISTOPHER BARKER IS THE SON OF THE CULT WRITER ELIZABETH Smart (*By Grand Central Station I Sat Down and Wept*) and the notorious poet, George Barker.

The Arms of the Infinite takes the reader inside the minds of both parents and, from their first fateful meeting and subsequent elopement, Barker candidly reveals their obsessive, passionate and volatile love affair.

He writes evocatively of his unconventional upbringing with his siblings in a shack in Ireland and, later, a rambling, falling-down house in Essex. Interesting and charismatic figures from the literary and art worlds are regular visitors and the book is full of fascinating cameos and anecdotes.

Barker is himself a gifted writer. An early draft of his memoir formed a cover story for the literary magazine, *Granta*.

• • •